Voices of Early Childhood Educators

CHILDHOOD STUDIES

Gaile S. Cannella
General Editor

Vol. 6

The Childhood Studies series is part of the Peter Lang Education list.
Every volume is peer reviewed and meets
the highest quality standards for content and production.

PETER LANG
New York • Bern • Frankfurt • Berlin
Brussels • Vienna • Oxford • Warsaw

Susan Bernheimer

Voices of Early
Childhood Educators

PETER LANG
New York • Bern • Frankfurt • Berlin
Brussels • Vienna • Oxford • Warsaw

Library of Congress Cataloging-in-Publication Data

Names: Bernheimer, Susan, author.
Title: Voices of early childhood educators / Susan Bernheimer.
Description: New York: Peter Lang, 2016.
Series: Childhood studies; vol. 6
ISSN 2379-934X (print) | ISSN 2379-9358 (online)
Includes bibliographical references and index.
Identifiers: LCCN 2016005901 | ISBN 978-1-4331-3061-8 (hardcover: alk. paper)
ISBN 978-1-4331-3060-1 (paperback: alk. paper) | ISBN 978-1-4539-1826-5 (e-book)
Subjects: LCSH: Early childhood teachers—United States.
Early childhood education—United States.
Classification: LCC LB1775.6 .B48 2016 | DDC 372.21—dc23
LC record available at https://lccn.loc.gov/2016005901

Bibliographic information published by **Die Deutsche Nationalbibliothek**.
Die Deutsche Nationalbibliothek lists this publication in the "Deutsche
Nationalbibliografie"; detailed bibliographic data are available
on the Internet at http://dnb.d-nb.de/.

The paper in this book meets the guidelines for permanence and durability
of the Committee on Production Guidelines for Book Longevity
of the Council of Library Resources.

"What can happen in a college class in early childhood education—and why should it? With vivid stories from her own teaching, Susan Bernheimer confirms what I too have discovered while teaching adults—that we learn most about human development by listening and sharing experiences with the many folks who are not like us. In an increasingly diverse world, that's basic to respectful, empathetic work with children and families."

Elizabeth Jones, Author of Teaching Adults Revisited:
Active Learning for Early Childhood Educators

"Susan Bernheimer says, 'Each student carries a story containing the seeds of new knowledge, including their struggles and challenges, fears and failures, and new forms of strength and wisdom. The particulars of their issues may differ with circumstance, but all describe a multitude of ways people are living amidst personal, familial, and societal challenges.' Sharing their own voices, the author describes how her students engage in the deep work of becoming not only more self-aware, but gaining better insights into the issues they will encounter in working with diverse children, families, and coworkers. This is a heartwarming and wise book. It deserves attention from all teacher educators."

Margie Carter, Co-author, Training Teachers: A Harvest of Theory and Practice

"Susan Bernheimer has made a contribution to human connectivity and a more global understanding, acceptance, and appreciation across linguistic, religious, and cultural boundaries. The subtlety and complexity of the students' paths and hence perspectives illuminated at a new depth the work we have to do to help facilitate and empower the teachers of young children in our contemporary global environment. Bernheimer's work is compassionate and transformative in her recounting, and especially in her willingness to share her own deep reflections on her reciprocal experience of growth and learning from those she facilitates."

Lee Turner Johnson, President,
Grantland Johnson Institute of Leadership Development

This book is dedicated to the many early childhood educators who are quietly working to bring about a more peaceful and viable future for our world. The stories recounted throughout the book represent the devotion and hard work of those who have chosen to be part of this critically needed and often invisible field. Their stories, unless otherwise requested, are presented anonymously in this book.

Contents

Acknowledgments

My deepest gratitude goes to the many early childhood educators whom I have had the privilege to know as students and colleagues. Their stories of courage and perseverance in the face of personal and professional challenges have inspired me to find an approach to education that honors their hard-earned wisdom. The importance of the stories in this book goes beyond particular events. Their gifts lay in the extraordinary honesty and invaluable insights they offer of personal and professional transformation.

My work of developing and implementing a new approach to preparing early childhood educators could not have taken place without the support of institutions of higher education. I want to thank the Los Angeles Community Colleges for allowing me the freedom to explore an alternative approach to education, thus enabling me to embrace and work with the many hidden gifts of our nontraditional students. I am indebted to Pacific Oaks College for supporting my use of pedagogical practice that extends far beyond the parameters of traditional education. It was a testament to their commitment of upholding a mission of social justice, which honors each student's life as an integral part of the learning process.

The concept upon which the storytelling practice in this book is based was built on the foundation of other early childhood educators who stepped outside accepted academic beliefs. I want to thank Elizabeth Jones, Margie Carter, Janet Gonzalez-Mena, Louise Derman-Sparks, and Lillian Katz for their insightful work in the field. I am grateful to the work and writings of Paulo Freire, which prompted me to create an empowering approach to education while teaching students from impoverished communities. Further enhancing my professional growth has been the annual Reconceptualizing Early Childhood International Conferences, which have provided a forum for ideas and practice at the cutting edge of our field. These have been greatly enhanced by my professional collaboration with Tim Sundeen.

The writing of this book could not have taken place without the dedicated help and support of others. Elizabeth (Betty) Jones combined her unique ability to be playful and fierce in her ongoing feedback, reading chapter after chapter, till we came to a place that pleased us both. My very good friend Jacqueline Green sat by my side over many years as the book unfolded, listening, offering brilliant insights, arguing about ideas, and always extending her support, as I hammered away at putting it all on paper. Who could have dreamed that a friendship that began in kindergarten would continue to blossom many decades later?

I would like to thank Anne Wood for her exceptional editing skills that have made such a difference to the quality of both my books. My dear friend Doris Lora also took on the role of using her remarkable editing skills with my completed manuscript. I could not have finished this book without the support and hard work of Frances Schireson, who formatted the references, and wrote and offered further editing feedback. I want to thank Jerry Cowart for his artistic talent, skill, and patience in working with me in formulating a design for the cover of this book.

Fortunately, during my long hours alone while writing this book, I was surrounded by a circle of precious friends. Thank you Jennifer Glaser, Vivian Rothstein, Sara Shane, Marsha Epstein, Stephanie

Pollard, and Donna Lambson for all your kindness, patience, and support. Beyond Los Angeles, but close to my heart, I want to thank my longtime friend Emmy Davis. In remembrance of two dear friends who have passed on, Eve Triffo and Sara Exposito, I am deeply grateful to have had you in my life.

Last, but certainly not least, I want to thank my children, David and Adina, who are now two of my closest friends as adults. Liam, my grandson, is only six, but he is truly my very good friend. I am lucky to have two loving and supportive siblings, Judy and Ben. And, I am forever grateful to have been raised by my parents, Leonard Schireson and Bea Wartell, who laid a foundation that honors life and family.

To those of you who are taking the time to read and ponder the ideas in this book, I extend my deepest gratitude. I can be reached at sbern21@gmail.com or via my website: www.susanbernheimer.com.

Foreword

Once upon a time the world of human beings was wild and rural and tribal. People lived in small communities—some nomadic, some settled, all family-based. They spoke different languages and developed different ceremonies. Sometimes they had trading relationships with the communities nearby; sometimes they attacked them on sight. Being different was a threat to the way things are supposed to be, for our people.

But many, many centuries later the whole world is living with the accumulated outcomes of endless human curiosity: What's this? How can I make it different? Invention, urbanization, technology—all these have obliterated most of the tidiness of living only with people like us. Like it or not, we repeatedly encounter diversity in its very many forms—people who don't talk like us, dress like us, believe what we believe, raise their children by our values. We can't even see or hear or touch many of these people—they're only part of our virtual environment, populating the World Wide Web. Exciting—but anxiety producing. How do we know what to do next?

Throughout human history, most young children have been cared for by members of their families, who had a lifelong investment in their well-being. They watched and participated in the activities of adults and older children, in their homes and neighborhoods. By being there, they learned their communities' stories, both literal—day-to-day—and mythical.

But what's happening now? In this book, early childhood educator Susan Bernheimer demands that we pay attention to the complexity of our greatly changed world and its continuing challenges to child-rearing. Many young children in the millennial United States are being cared for not by their families but by strangers—persons with no long-term personal investment in their past and their future. In such a society, what are the sources of commitment to other people's children?

To care well for children, we have to build relationships with them by establishing trust and love and by discovering shared pleasures. We know what we want them to be—speaking our language, learning our stories, sharing responsibility for living in our world and loving us. Sometimes we make new discoveries together. New discoveries enliven our lives, unless they contradict the ways we know things are supposed to be.

When we encounter people who are different from us, how do we react? Human diversity is about different perspectives. Different perspectives can be both interesting and difficult.

Interesting: Tourist curriculum. "Oh, how quaint! How delicious!" Pleasantly surprising. A chance for a night out. Not trying to take the perspective of the other, but simply finding it entertaining, even weird. The international district in a big city is a fascinating place to get together for an evening.

Difficult: When you have to live and work with each other, differences can be offensive. When I am caring for your child, your precious child, differences can even feel threatening. We don't agree on what that child needs, and I know I'm right because I'm a professional and you're only her mama. Of course you shouldn't spoon-feed a four-year old, she needs to be independent. Of course you shouldn't be speaking Spanish to her, this is the United States.

Learning to be a professional, in early childhood education, is about learning to build authentic relationships with people who may not be very much like us. We don't learn that by reading a book about other cultures' holidays. We learn it through practice, through sharing personal stories with real people. Stories we tell ourselves are a setting for inner reflection. Stories we hear from others challenge us to rethink our assumptions about how life works, and they expand our working theories of human development.

This is a book of stories by a college teacher committed to this perspective. It offers a paradigm for learning about early childhood education, in the day-to-day stories shared by the amazingly diverse students who enroll in her classes. In those classes, they are expected to learn from reflection on others' experiences and on their own. Really? That really happened in your life? And then what did you do? Where did you learn to do that?

Personal narrative is the glue that holds a human community together. It's the way in which its members embed their knowing in their own and others' experiences. It's a basic skill to be learned by young children—learned from their elders, and from their playmates, and from the legends and books that their people return to again and again, to construct meaning in their lives. It's a lot harder to learn in a contemporary child care center than it was in an extended family long ago.

Caring for children and families requires relationships. Relationships are built through story sharing. Relationship building with persons different from oneself requires lots of purposeful practice. In the classes described in this book, that's what happens.

Susan is inviting her readers to learn from her students' stories, just as their classmates do—and just as she does. How are their stories like yours? How are they different? Do you experience different as wrong? And wouldn't it all be easier if there weren't so much diversity in our lives?

But would it be as interesting?

Elizabeth Jones

Faculty Emerita

Pacific Oaks College

Introduction

The stories you are about to read bring to life the volatile, changing dynamics of modern times. These are times in which traditional communities and rules for living have given way to vast movements of people, shifting ideas, and intermingling of cultures. In such times, many established beliefs about family life and ways of raising children are no longer viable options. Working parents, people living in unfamiliar communities, and migrating families all require a place to care for their children. Child care institutions have taken on this new role in our society. It is a world filled with hidden complications and emotionally intense encounters. It is within this ever-changing and complex world that early childhood educators must be prepared to provide support and services needed by children and parents today.

Over the past decades, social, political, and economic forces have added to the complexity of child care institutions. More children immersed in a language they don't understand. Children with families in strife. Distraught parents. Anxious teachers facing overwhelming demands. Where to start? What to do? These are questions that have weighed on my mind as I watched early childhood professionals

silently grappling for answers, trying to cope with increasingly difficult challenges.

This book is a culmination of my years working in the field of early
childhood education. I began by working with young children and
moved into teaching adults who care for and teach young children. As
a community college instructor, I often felt haunted by students' stories of frustration and their struggles in dealing with troubled parents,
language barriers, conflicts with co-workers, and children coming to
school tired and hungry.

It was while teaching in programs serving students in poverty
that I became increasingly aware of the need to expand my approach
to teacher preparation. Textbook learning theories, lectures, project
assignments, and testing were not working for these students. Theories
often did not apply to their life circumstances, and they even labeled
their kind of life as damaged and unhealthy. As I witnessed students'
struggles to connect with the material, I searched for meaningful ways
of reaching them.

I began inviting students to share their personal stories as a key part
of the learning process. As students' lives became part of our curriculum, a larger world entered the classroom. I started to understand the
inner side of events I had heard in the news, the gravity of their struggles, and unexpected forms of resilience. Their stories, like canaries in
a coal mine exposing, and exposed to, unseen dangers, demonstrated
a critical need to expand our approach to preparing teachers (Bernheimer, 2003). This was the beginning of my recognizing the importance of students' stories as a lens into the changing dynamics and new
challenges facing our field.

Early Childhood Education Today

Early childhood education is part of a world that is rapidly coming
together in new ways, forging complex relationships amidst diverse
populations. By its very nature, it is a field that is inclusive. All children deserve programs that provide safety, understanding, and support of their optimal potential. This mandate of inclusivity must begin

by embracing the diversity of our children and their teachers. It is a mandate that calls into question information, theories, and guidelines that exclude populations of children and teachers. Such a mandate demands ongoing questioning, revision, and revitalization of a field dedicated to a relevant education built on principles of social justice and inclusivity.

Amir is representative of a growing population of children caught in a jumble of complicated arrangements. At age five he spends his early mornings at home with his family, speaking Farsi. He then goes to child care for two hours with children speaking English, Spanish, and Farsi. He will then attend an academic, English-speaking kindergarten class followed by three hours in child care mixed with older children. Each situation demands adjustment to different children, adults, languages, styles of learning, and expectations.

Teachers, like children, experience diversity as they are drawn to early childhood education from all parts of our society. Older women returning to the workplace, immigrant and minority women from impoverished communities, men looking for meaningful work, and young women searching for a career all come together in their desire to teach and care for children.

Through the stories and struggles of college students and practitioners, this book will examine the many faces of early childhood education today: young, inexperienced students; older, returning students; early childhood teachers and directors; and educators dedicated to preparing future and current teachers. It invites early childhood educators to read others' stories and learn from the questions they raise. If you're preparing to enter the field, this book takes you backstage to see what's happening on the job, and what others' experience in getting there has been.

The Road Ahead

New circumstances call for new answers. These can only emerge as we allow unanswered questions to take us into unexplored territory. Paulo Freire (1998), in his work as an educator and philosopher, asserted that we should always be expecting new knowledge to arise, transcending the old, enabling us to move beyond the current limitations of conditioned knowledge that we have produced.

Working in early childhood education, with children, parents, and adult team members, is not just a matter of information and technique. It is a matter of relationship with self and others, and it calls for learning that acknowledges the personal world of inner reflection, feelings, and motivation. This happens through our stories—yours, those of your colleagues, and the stories of the early childhood practitioners in this book. Effective work with children is both a public and private activity, demanding personal narrative and the ability to analyze general knowledge. Stories bring these two essential components together (Bernheimer, 2003; Clark and Rossiter, 2008; Cranton, 2006).

The stories and personal narratives in this book will take us on a journey that covers the rocky terrain of self-awareness, bringing voice to hidden worlds and crossing borders of differing realities. It is a journey designed to bring the field of early childhood education back home to its rightful legacy of honoring the full scope of our human experience—and of bringing our children into a world of hope and justice.

References

Bernheimer, S. (2003). *New possibilities for early childhood education: Stories from our nontraditional students*. New York: Peter Lang.

Clark, M. C., & Rossiter, M. (2008). Narrative learning in adult life. *New Directions for Adult and Continuing Education, 2008*(119), 61–70.

Cranton, P. (2006). *Understanding and promoting transformative learning: A guide for educators of adults*. San Francisco: Jossey-Bass.

Freire, P. (1998). Pedagogy of the oppressed: The fear of freedom. In A. Freire & D. Macedo (Eds.), *The Paulo Freire reader* (pp. 45–66). New York: Continuum.

Chapter 1

Child Care: An Institution at Risk

Sitting in my office, I hear the sound of cars in the parking lot as students leave for the evening. It's 10:30 p.m. and the college will soon be closing for the night. It's hard for me to leave. I keep looking over my notes from our class. I feel both pleased and disturbed.

Tonight was our first session of this upper-division class, Understanding Children and Parents. There was an air of excitement. The students appeared passionate about being in the field and learning more about it. Their introductions gave everybody a chance to be an active part of the class and an opportunity to get to know each other. It also provided a valuable way for me to gain a clearer sense of their needs as early childhood educators.

The disturbing part of the evening came as I listened to students' response to my question, "What would you like to get out of taking this class?" As we went around the room, the emotion behind their comments included much frustration and anger. Beneath their varied statements was a common message—a feeling that they were ill-equipped for the unexpected challenges they were facing as teachers and directors in child care programs. I was surprised at the degree of difficulty they were encountering. As upper-division students, they had studied theories of development, age-appropriate curriculums, multicultural education, and communication with parents. Why did they feel so frustrated?

Beneath the Surface

Recently, I visited a well-established child care program whose director had asked me for a consultation. Walking through the front door, I saw lovely images of a safe and happy place for children. The walls were covered with posters of children smiling and playing. The sign-in table had fresh flowers on it. Entering the director's office, I noticed it was filled with stuffed animals.

"How would you describe this center?" I asked Barbara. "We are like a family," she answered. "What does that mean to you?" I asked. She thought for a moment and said, "We are people who have something in common and children are a part of it." "I like that," I said. "What is it that you want my help with?" "Conflicts," she said. "Staff members have trouble with each other. Parents criticize staff. Some parents don't like our play-based curriculum; they want to see more traditional academic learning." I questioned her, grinning, "Don't most families have conflicts?" "I guess so," she agreed. "But when parents and staff don't like it here, they often leave. Our turnover is too high."

Over the next several months, I would gain a deeper look into the largely unseen reality of the child care center. It soon became apparent that the outer simplicity of daily care belies the true nature of this highly complex service. Beneath the carefully calculated picture of calm predictability with its reassuring schedules, classrooms, and smiling teachers, I came to see the unsettled reality of a vulnerable institution sitting at the crux of a changing society.

Regardless of its image, the child care program is not the child's real family. It is an institution that provides a service for families who are in need of care for their children. Parents are leaving their infants and children in the care of strangers, which is a process filled with anxiety and vulnerability.

The child care center as a business carries a different set of priorities from its ideal as a family. In direct contrast to the fluid, soft world of family-like staff/child interactions are the hard, accountable demands of business and legal liability. My observations revealed the volatile and delicate dynamics that lie just beneath the surface of a family picture. Every day I saw teachers involved in highly interactive, emotionally charged roles with each other, the children, and the parents.

Everyday Risks of Child Care

As caregivers of young children, the staff must be prepared to respond skillfully to a constant flow of unexpected situations. This must be accomplished under the close scrutiny of supervisors, peers, and parents.

Risks with Children

In the playground one morning, I see firsthand the pressure of needing to perform in an environment of high visibility. Watching from a bench, I notice a two-year-old girl sitting in the sand area behind a boy who is busy digging a large hole. She stops her own sand play and begins looking at the boy's shoulder. Suddenly she opens her mouth and bites him. Hearing his screams, a teacher runs over to them. Holding the girl's face to see the wound on the boy, she firmly tells her, "See, you hurt him. You need to use your words." A short time later, the same girl bites another child near the slide. As the teacher runs over, two other staff members follow her. This time, the teacher has an angry tone in her voice. The two teachers watch as she handles the situation. Their physical presence sends a clear message of distrust in the teacher's ability to supervise this child. The teacher looks very anxious, knowing there will be further consequences with the parents of these children and with her own supervisor. The family theme has suddenly become part of the unspoken professional dangers in their work.

Risks with Parents

Each day the unpredictable nature of this institution grows. Teachers are not just on display with the parents, director, and each other, they must also carefully balance attachment and intimacy with detachment and professionalism. Parents monitor and judge the quality of the program.

Parent trust can easily turn to suspicion and anger. For parents, there are ever-present, unspoken questions, fears, and guilt lurking in the background. What if something happens to my child? Is my child really being well cared for? The blurred boundaries of teachers in a parental role create an ongoing potential for difficulties. The fragility of this relationship erupts one evening as I watch parents picking up their children. The reception area starts filling with parents and children hugging and talking as they reunite after a long day. Several exhausted children are crying as parents, equally exhausted, try to get them out quickly.

In the middle of this activity, a man comes tearing across the area, quickly entering the toddler room. Everyone hears him screaming, "How dare you release my son to his stepfather. I'm the father, do you understand? I'm the father! Don't you ever let my child go with him again. Do you hear me?" Soon the teacher comes out shaking with fear as the father continues screaming at her. Barbara runs over and tries to calm down the situation. As the father turns on Barbara, I watch the tension on their faces while they attempt to maintain a loving atmosphere while being caught in a painful family drama and demeaning treatment.

Risks of Leadership

I observed the ways that Barbara tries to deal with ongoing, complicated issues with staff, children, and parents. She is attempting to balance a fragile system filled with conflicting needs. Her position often requires her to make difficult decisions that will please one faction but not the other.

Barbara's philosophy of leadership fits into her ideal concept of a democratic family. She says, "Who am I, as a director, to tell them what or how to do it? As a team, they are more likely to be responsible. The more I give them leadership, the more they own it." Yet, the same qualities she uses to express a family concept, such as caring and acceptance, often result in a lack of resolution of problematic issues.

Margaret, the receptionist, tells me she "sees and hears a lot of what's going on here." She says, "There's a lot of negativity with staff and a lack of communication with Barbara." Margaret adds, "Some teachers feel she always sides with parents when there is a conflict. And she doesn't deal with our problems. Whenever we tell her something is wrong, she just pats us and says that everything will get better." Beneath Margaret's report of discontent sits a dangerous undercurrent of the unmet family ideal.

Barbara is responsible for running a business, maintaining regulations, supervising, and training staff. She also believes that it is important for her to uphold a vision of a loving family. Yet, putting this into practice requires the director to cultivate a partnership and common vision among the teachers (Carter and Curtis, 2009), a task that Barbara has not yet accomplished. Adding to the inherent challenges of operating a child care program are the unexpected ways that current societal issues intrude upon their role of attending to the needs of children.

Political and Social Issues Enter Child Care

Child care programs generally bring forth the picture of a protected environment far from the harsh reality of politics. The history of early childhood movements tells a very different story. From its beginning, this field has been used to fulfill a variety of societal agendas, ranging from religious, philosophical, political, and industrial to scientific and technological issues (Cochron, 2011; Beatty, 1995). What happens when programs are caught between their educational knowledge and current societal beliefs? What happens when unresolved social and political issues enter the classroom?

When Barbara became director three years ago, she shifted from an academic program to a "play to learn" curriculum based on developmental needs. About half the parents took their children out. Barbara has attempted to counteract this pressure from parents by having her teachers elaborate on the academic benefits of every activity the children are engaged in.

Barbara tells me that just last week a new parent wanted to know what her child is learning. She said, "Billy is already two and half years old and still does not know how to write his name. He should be counting higher numbers, and needs to know all his colors before turning three years." Barbara told the parent he is learning the motor and cognitive skills needed to master reading, writing, and counting. The parent said that this was not enough and left the center.

The pressure parents experience is not without reason. They are worried about how their child will do with our latest national agenda of competency-based programs and standardized testing. They know their child will be expected to pass these tests, beginning in kindergarten. I sense Barbara's frustration as she tries to hold onto a program that fits her educational beliefs amidst our latest societal pressures.

War Enters the Classroom

Other problematic areas feel more immediate and urgent. Involvement in a war thousands of miles away is finding its way into the child care classroom. Aaron was just turning four when he started at the child care center. Aaron's mother sits in Barbara's office telling her about her son's background. His father had completed two tours of duty in Afghanistan. The first took place when she was pregnant with Aaron. When Aaron was one, his father went back again for a second tour. He returned when Aaron was two and a half. One month after returning, he was killed in a motorcycle accident. The mother tells this devastating story with little emotion. Feeling concerned, Barbara asks how they are doing. The mother becomes very guarded, and replies, "We're doing very well. I'm taking good care of Aaron and I just found a job that I like." After their talk, Barbara tells me she is worried about their situation. She alerts the teachers in Aaron's class.

A few weeks later, I see Aaron in his new class. He seems excited and interested in everything. His teachers tell me they are very pleased with how well he is adjusting. Their only concern is that he is a little aggressive and never mentions his father. After several months, Barbara is very worried about mother and son. The mother has lost a lot of weight, and Aaron is becoming more withdrawn. His teachers work with Aaron to express himself. They keep asking his mother how she is doing, and she tells them everything is fine.

Barbara decides to have a meeting with her. She mentions she is concerned about how thin she has become. The mother laughs it off. She says, "There is nobody to cook for, so I just don't eat. Aaron only eats hot dogs, chicken nuggets, and macaroni and cheese. I don't have anybody to cook for, so I just don't eat." Alarmed, Barbara asks if she is getting any support or has somebody to talk to. The mother quickly says that she is doing just fine. Barbara suggests several people she could go to, but the mother is not interested. After the mother leaves, Barbara tells me she is frightened for the mother and child and is not sure what to do about it.

Problematic societal issues do not always present themselves as clearly as fear for a child's academic success or the repercussions of war. They often weave their way into child care centers in subtle ways that can leave staff shocked and defensive with families they are serving.

Cultural Clashes with Parents

Child care programs are not protected from the prejudices and misunderstandings of our society. Cultural conflicts with parents can be particularly hard on a young child's well-being. Young children are in a process of bonding with their parents and with their caregivers (Gonzalez-Mena, 2007). What happens when a teacher's educational beliefs become a barrier to understanding the needs of parents?

Dominic is 22 years old and is a teacher in the toddler room. He has completed 24 units in early childhood education and has worked in the field for several years. He is knowledgeable about developmental stages, and his interactions with children are responsive and caring. Barbara feels very lucky to have him at the center. In addition to being a good teacher, Dominic is male and Latino. She feels he is a good role model and can relate well to minority cultures.

I watch Dominic and agree that he is an excellent teacher. He interacts well with the children and his program provides the needed motor/sensory activities that are very important for this age group. Mona, an 18-month-old African American girl, has recently joined his class. Mona's mother is very happy to have found this program. She is a single working parent who is also going to school to become a nurse. Visiting the toddler playground, I often see her daughter on the yard gloriously playing in the sandbox. She seems to have adjusted well to the program.

After a few weeks, her mother comes in looking very upset when she sees Mona. I hear her saying, "Look at your hair. It's full of sand again. I told you to stop playing in the sandbox." Clearly angry, she turns to Dominic. She tells him that she does not want Mona to play in the sandbox anymore. Dominic asks her why. The mother responds that when Mona gets sand in her hair, it takes her hours to get it out. Dominic patiently explains how important sensory play is at this age and that it will interfere with Mona's full development if she cannot play in the sandbox. He adds that Mona especially loves the sandbox. Dominic tells her that even though he knows she is busy, he feels it is worth spending some extra time in order to let Mona have this experience.

I listen as the conversation goes back and forth for 20 minutes. Finally, the mother says, "If Mona goes into the sandbox again, I'm taking her out of the program." Dominic looks confused and upset. He decides to talk with the director. Barbara tries to patiently explain the importance of considering the needs of the parent. She feels the mother is looking to Dominic to help her find a way that can work. She tells him that she has come across this problem before—the texture of African American hair makes it difficult to remove the sand. She suggests using a net or shower cap when the child plays in the sandbox.

This is not what Dominic expected to hear. He quickly lets her know he does not agree, "Why are we going to go through all this, just so Mona can play in the sandbox? What if other parents demand their children wear gloves whenever they paint?" Barbara remains firm, "The mother is under a lot of stress, and crying out for help. We are going to do this. You need to work it out." Dominic is not happy as he finds himself caught between his theoretical knowledge and the need to support this parent and child.

Cultural bias and misunderstandings can become intensely emotional when they occur between two teachers. This is an area of particular vulnerability for teachers who must work in close partnership for an extended period every day. In such cases, subtle differences of verbal tones, mannerisms, and cultural beliefs can create ongoing emotional distress and an inability to effectively care for children.

Cultural Clash in the Classroom

Teachers bring with them their personal experiences, ways of communicating, culture, and biases into their working partnerships. Under the demanding work of carrying for infants and young children, small differences can escalate into serious problems.

In the infant room there are five people on staff. One teacher is white American, two teachers are Latina, and two are Armenian. They work together eight hours a day. The center wants to use the home language of the child, so teachers often speak in their native language with an infant, parent, and each other. As they navigate the intimate world of caring for infants, Barbara tells me they go through continual personal and cultural clashes: "When the teachers speak in their native language, the others feel they are being talked about and don't like it. And things have been getting increasingly tense between Gina (Latina) and Mora (Armenian)."

While sitting in Barbara's office one day, Gina comes rushing in looking very upset. She blurts out, "That's it. I can't work with her anymore. I just said to Mora, 'Make sure you change the sheets for the babies.' That's all! And she comes right up to my face and yells,

'I already did.' I'm not going to be treated this way!" Barbara tries to calm Gina down, "This is just the way her culture communicates. Every culture has a different way of communicating. In some, people get very close and talk loud. It is not a personal attack." Barbara adds soothingly, "You're both doing a good job taking care of the children, and that's what it is all about."

Gina starts to cry, repeating, "I'm not going to be treated that way," and storms out of the office. As she leaves, Mora comes in telling Barbara that she is constantly being told what to do by Gina, adding, "Gina does not trust me. That's why she's always shouting orders at me." Barbara tries to explain that some cultures view caring for infants in a more protective manner and worry about everything being done right. It is not a personal attack. Dissatisfied Mora marches out of the office with an angry look on her face. Barbara turns to me like a frustrated mother, "I don't know what to do. They just keep fighting, even though I tell them these are only cultural differences."

Barbara is face-to-face with the baffling array of complex and subtle differences that permeate child care programs in a highly diverse society. Addressing such issues requires finding ways to acknowledge and confront the barriers of prejudice and misunderstanding that arise in a myriad of forms in settings caring for children (Derman-Sparks & Olsen Edwards, 2012). For Barbara, like many early childhood professionals, this is a highly challenging and frustrating task.

Emergence of a New Story

Leaving the center, I think of Bateson's insight about living in modern times, "The quality of improvisation characterizes more and more lives today, lived in uncertainty, full of the inklings of alternatives. In a rapidly changing and interdependent world, single models are less likely to be viable and plans more likely to go awry" (Bateson, 1995, p. 8). I am reminded of the endless number of times the staff of this center was required to make quick, unexpected decisions based only on inklings or partial knowledge.

Every day, I watched the teachers and the director face innumerable challenges in their quest to create a "new societal family." Because problems occur with no warning and have uncertain solutions, they have to respond quickly to situations, many of which could have serious repercussions. Within this uncertain milieu, they need to connect with others across cultures, philosophies, race, age, gender, personality, and differing socioeconomic backgrounds. These connections often include unresolved issues, unclear answers, and subtle conflicts. On a daily basis, I observed the staff experiencing the disequilibrium of life at the forefront of modern society.

My Next Journey

On my way out, I glance back at the children happily running through the playground. Several teachers smile and wave at me. Children are coming to the fence to say good-bye. I am struck by the uniquely precious quality of the child care institution in our society. Amidst the rush of a bustling metropolitan city, a world of political fighting, wars, and social upheaval, the child care center provides a place dedicated to caring for our young, our most vulnerable population.

I have also become acutely aware that child care centers do not match our ideal picture of the protected environment, untouched by the world's problems. Nor is it a place where teachers earn an easy living by watching children as they lounge together in the sunshine. I am more convinced than ever that this is an institution functioning at the crux of modern-day political and social upheaval. I have witnessed the truth that programs for children are part of the historical and social dynamics of their time and are built upon hidden assumptions and beliefs that are taken for granted (Tobin, Hsueh, & Karasawa, 2009; Weber, 1984).

It was through an ethnographic approach of daily observations, discussions with staff, written notes, and personal reflection that I was able to gain further insights into the underlying dynamics of child care today. As early as the 1970s, Heath (1983) wrote of the need to make use of this type of comprehensive approach to teacher preparation. She was clear that desegregation with its new challenges of diversity would require an educational pedagogy that included ways of accessing both inner and outer knowledge. Forty years later, I brought my own confirmation of Heath's words back into the classroom.

References

Bateson, M. (1995). *Peripheral visions: Learning along the way.* New York: Harper Perennial.

Beatty, B. (1995). *Preschool education in America: The culture of young children from the colonial era to the present.* New Haven, CT: Yale University Press.

Carter, M., & Curtis, D. (2009). *The visionary director: A handbook for dreaming, organizing and improving your center* (2nd ed.). St. Paul, MN: Redleaf Press.

Cochron, M. (2011). International perspectives on early childhood education. *Educational Policy, 25,* 65–91.

Derman-Sparks, L., & Olsen Edwards, J. (2012). *Anti-bias for young children and ourselves.* Washington, DC: National Association for the Education of Young Children.

Gonzalez-Mena, J. (2007). *Diversity in early care and education: Honoring differences* (5th ed.). Dubuque, IA: McGraw-Hill Education.

Heath, S. B. (1983). *Ways with words: Language, life and work in communities and classrooms.* Cambridge: Cambridge University Press.

Tobin, J., Hsueh, Y., & Karasawa, M. (2009). *Preschool in three cultures revisited: China, Japan, and the United States.* Chicago: University of Chicago Press.

Weber, E. (1984). *Ideas influencing early childhood education: A theoretical analysis.* New York: Teachers College Press.

Chapter 2

Illuminating Hidden Worlds

Students are smiling and nodding as I enter the classroom. This is the fourth week of our class on understanding children and parents. Twenty-two students are sitting around a long rectangular table; many are chatting with others sitting nearby. Since the class meets at 7:00 p.m. and most of the students have already completed a long day of work, some look tired. The students are highly diverse, including Caucasians, Hispanics, African Americans, Asians, and several from Middle Eastern countries. Although the majority are in their thirties and forties, their ages range from early twenties to mid-sixties.

Interactions among the students are congenial and caring. This was not always the case. When the class began, students were sitting with anxious looks on their faces or busy checking electronic devices. Watching their uneasy silence reminded me there was important work ahead as we started our new semester.

Storytelling in Action

Looking back at our first evening together, my purpose was to create a safe environment and a context for personal sharing. I began the class by saying we would go around the room and each share something about ourselves, including a story of our name. I started with my own story. After sharing my background, I described the saga of my last name. Beginning with my maiden name, I unfolded layer upon layer of name changes as I moved through a marriage, divorce, and shifting social etiquette. Along with the resulting name changes, I attended several colleges as an undergraduate, and several more as a graduate student—each under a different name. Everybody began laughing as I described the resulting chaos each time I attempted to locate past educational records.

My sharing revealed more than the story of my name. It provided a glimpse into the tumultuous social and educational dynamics that were part of my personal history. Most important, I was setting up a safe context for me to engage in mutual dialogue with students. I noticed a similar dynamic taking place among the students.

Telling the story of our names in that first class began the process of breaking down students' isolation. Everybody's interest grew as each student shared his or her story. Already hidden worlds began to emerge: Cindy's hyphenated surname reflected her choice of an interracial marriage; Mary was named after a great-grandmother who had worked as a slave; Maribel found out her father named her after a favorite cat he had as a child. Whether poignant or funny, our common humanity emerged along with our diversity. These two opposing dimensions— our common humanity and our diversity—became an underlying theme throughout the semester.

One of the critical goals of this class is developing the kind of sensitivity needed to build trusting relationships across multiple differences (Bernheimer & Jones, 2013). Sharing stories begins this type of learning. Through stories, we are weaving together learning concepts with students' personal experiences, reflections, and dialogues. Combined, they bring forth the understanding needed for navigating the complicated relationships they will encounter in child care settings.

Storytelling in a variety of formats is one of the key educational modalities I will be using to create a more comprehensive curriculum. Moon and Flower (2008) believe that stories engage students in a wide-ranging form of learning.

> Story can capture the holistic and lived experience of the subject being taught; it can tap into imagination, emotions, and form new and meaningful connections between existing areas of knowledge. (p. 232)

Unexpected Story

Now in our fourth meeting, students are familiar with our custom of beginning class with presentations from their biographical story assignment. In addition to a written biography, students create a symbolic persona doll (Derman-Sparks & ABC Task Force, 1989) representing their personal development within the cultural context of their lives. After greeting the class, I announce that we will have our first presentation. The room becomes silent and alert. Everyone waits with hushed expectation.

Melissa stands in front of the class holding a Velcro board with four stick figures of varying sizes. Next to her is a large bag. She is Caucasian with blond hair and the kind of natural beauty often seen in advertisements for skin or hair products. A 28-year-old preschool teacher, she is taking courses towards her bachelor's degree. Everybody is watching attentively as she introduces herself to the class. Holding the board in front of her, she begins her presentation.

Melissa describes her early life growing up on a ranch in Arizona as part of an intact family with three children and a family dog. Her story sounds idyllic as she talks of playing in the fields with her younger sister, she remembers adventures at a nearby river with their older brother, and recalls family barbecues in the evening. Her face clouds over as she tells us about the horror of seeing her dog, Charlie, run over by a car in front of their home. Melissa was six at the time. As she talks, she bends down a small, dark stick figure on the board.

Two years later, at eight, Melissa's younger sister became seriously ill. With a shaking voice, she shares the story of her sister's illness and death, bending down another stick figure. This tragedy had devastating repercussions on her family, and after several years her parents divorced. Her father sold the ranch and remarried. Melissa moved with her mother and brother to Los Angeles. Although they stayed in contact, Melissa seldom saw her father after they moved. She quietly bends down another stick figure. She continues her tale of increasing hardship. At 15, her older brother, tired of living in a small apartment with a mother working full-time, moved back to Arizona to live with his father. Melissa bends down another stick figure and stops talking. Looking around the room on the verge of tears, she adds, "I felt like nobody really cared about me. I stopped caring too." She continues, "During my high school years, I became rebellious and did poorly in school. I started drinking and using drugs. I couldn't deal with all the feelings coming up."

I see students with tears in their eyes as they listen to this unexpected story. Everyone is silently afraid of what will come next. But her story begins to change. At 15 she started working in a vocational education program helping to care for young children. A passion was growing in her.

By 16, she found new meaning in her life and was spending her time after school in the child care program. At 17, she fell in love with a boy in her class. They married right after graduation. This was not a fleeting young love. She describes their devotion to each other and the quick arrival of two children. She tells of overcoming many struggles as they continued their education while raising their children. Smiling, Melissa opens the large bag and brings out a tree with branches representing members of her family.

Following our procedure at the end of each presentation, students share their experience of listening to her story. Several just say thank you. Others share their amazement that she could find a good life after so much tragedy. Slowly some students express ways their perceptions were altered. Mary says, "You've been through so much. I'd never have known it by looking at you. You're so pretty." It's Shirley, an African American woman, who bluntly says, "You know, I thought you probably had the perfect life because you're white and pretty. All this time I was looking at you like you're some privileged white girl. So thank you for teaching me that I don't know anybody by just looking at them."

Both Melissa and Shirley appear to be on the verge of tears. I'm noticing a few students glancing at me for reassurance as a sense of disorientation permeates the room. I know this is a critical moment, one filled with great vulnerability for the two students and the class as a whole. The intensity of emotions and discomfort is a sign that Melissa's story has touched upon deep-seated issues. It also reflects how Melissa's "individual story" is illuminating a bigger, more secretive story enveloping our society. I am grateful for their courage in allowing these truths to come out.

As the room remains silent, I keep my own respectful silence with them. We are learning to welcome both silence and speech. The silence today is a way of honoring and reflecting upon this unexpected story, the honesty of student responses, and its impact on our perceptions. I don't want this moment to be swallowed up in a quickly moving agenda. I am reminded of Palmer's (2007) conviction that an educational space should be both hospitable and "charged." He writes of the need to offer nourishment while allowing students to feel the risks that are part of pursuing a deeper understanding of the world. I know the students need moments of risk, such as this, to prepare them for the deeper levels of inquiry we will engage in throughout our course.

I let Melissa know how much I appreciate her sharing the complicated and painful changes that took place in her family as they faced the crises of death and divorce. I acknowledge her courage of going beyond appearances to the real emotional struggles and strengths that are part of her unique journey. I emphasize how her story is helping everyone to understand a person's life beyond common stereotypical perceptions.

It is during these highly charged moments that my response can be a catalyst to deeper understanding and a willingness to risk sharing truths about their lives. I am reminded of the importance of creating an atmosphere conducive to receiving and accepting differing paths and forms of reality. Brownlee and Berthelsen (2005) discuss the value of having a supportive and empathetic environment, in which cognitive and affective dimensions of learning come together. They believe the very act of learning is an emotional affair, particularly if students are being asked to reflect upon and reconstruct previous beliefs.

Listening to Melissa reinforces the importance of understanding the whole of a person's life (Dominice, 2000). Her narrative story is moving us into hidden beliefs and painful emotions of students' lives that often remain largely unnoticed in classroom learning. Their stories are teaching everyone that development is a complex, multifaceted process: "In real stories, there are often no clear answers, people make mistakes, explore different solutions to life's problems, and discover unexpected strength and resilience from difficult as well as positive experiences" (Bernheimer, 2005, p. 82).

Every student carries a story containing the seeds of new knowledge, including their struggles and challenges, fears and failures, and new forms of strength and wisdom. The particulars of their stories may differ with the circumstances, but all describe a multitude of ways people are living amidst personal, familial, and societal challenges.

Observing Others and Self

I emphasize that students will need to become careful observers of others and of themselves. The observation assignment requires students to observe children and adults in action. This includes selecting children that represent at least one type of diversity that is different from their own background of race, culture, socioeconomic level, and mental or physical abilities. They are asked to watch for interactions that reflect important issues, such as power dynamics, diversity, communication, and bias.

An important part of the assignment poses questions that require careful attention to their own reactions as they are observing. Questions include the following: Are you an insider or an outsider in this situation? What do you feel judgmental about? What do you approve of? The assignment is intended to deepen students' ability to be observant of both others and themselves.

Following the presentations, I discuss the observation assignment that is due today, and the importance of these skills in their work as early childhood educators. Students then form small groups and begin sharing from their observation experiences. Walking around the room, I hear lively conversations as they describe positive and negative observations. In one group, Amanda is talking about her observation of a kindergarten class in a low-income neighborhood. The children are Latino, Filipino, and African American. Half way through the morning, two new children are brought into the class. The principal tells the teacher they are both immigrants from Mexico and can only speak Spanish. He quickly leaves the classroom. Left behind are a frustrated looking teacher and two frightened children.

Amanda observes the class throughout the day. The teacher appears to make little effort to help these two children understand what is happening. Both children seem lost and sit watching others most of the time. At the end of the day, the teacher comes up to Amanda and tells her how frustrated she is in getting these children in the middle of the semester. She tells her that she is already stressed trying to prepare the children for upcoming standardized tests.

Initially, Amanda feels sympathy for the teacher. But, her sympathy turns to shock and anger when the teacher tells her she is bilingual but does not want to use her time translating for the children. She says that she will probably recommend that they be put into special education because their English is not adequately developed. Amanda speaks with intense anger and disbelief about this situation.

The group becomes engaged in a passionate discussion. Some students agree with Amanda, expressing their shock and outrage. Jane describes how upset she is hearing about a teacher who cares more about tests than the children. She continues with intense emotion, "What about the children? Doesn't anybody care about them? Don't they think about what it must be like to not understand anything and nobody is helping them?"

Other students join in with empathy for the teacher. Marjory says that she understands the teacher's view of this situation. She has also been under pressure to achieve a list of competencies for children in her four-year-old class. She talks about how hard it is when she has many children who hardly speak English. Making it even more stressful is that her own performance is evaluated by how well the children in her class do on the competencies. As the discussion progresses, it becomes more nuanced as students start seeing how complicated the issues are for this teacher.

Lillian shares that she is becoming more aware of how frightening it is for immigrant children and parents in her class. She keeps looking for ways to build links with parents and children, including posting family pictures at the entrance. She asked parents to bring in dress-up clothes from home for dramatics play, including cooking tools and instruments from their home countries. Lillian quietly adds that she still can't really communicate with most of the parents because they don't speak English.

Jeff, an attentive and calm Caucasian male, shares an observation that began negatively but later turned positive. He describes observing a classroom made up of four-year-old African American children and an African American teacher. He was upset watching how this teacher interacted with the children, "She was like a dictator, barking orders at them. She expected them to listen to every word she said, and pounced upon anyone not listening."

He explains that it was against all his beliefs about giving children lots of freedom to make their own choices and not telling them what to do. He then adds, "As I watched the class throughout the morning, I was shocked. The children seemed very happy, and they clearly loved this teacher. I really saw how I was an outsider, and was judging them from my own beliefs." Several students remind him that this kind of style of teaching was written about by Lisa Delpit (2006). He said that he remembered this once he calmed down. But initially his emotions and opinions just took over.

I'm pleased to hear both the honesty and exploration in their conversations. These types of discussions are designed to do more than share information. McDrury and Alterio (2002) point out the value of having several listeners view a story from multiple perspectives, since this kind of interaction increases "the opportunity to uncover new and possibly totally unexpected learning" (p. 54). This is a skill they will need in their work with children and families.

Facing an Uncertain World

Finding themselves at the crux of complicated social and political issues is not the picture most students have when they enter the field of early childhood education. As Mary said during a class discussion,

> I just want to take care of children. But its feeling too complicated and I'm not sure what to do anymore. I never expected to be dealing with parents battling over their children, immigrants who can't speak English, traumatized children, and co-workers who get angry every time I try to do something creative. I know what children need. I feel so stressed out trying to get this across to parents, and even some of my co-workers. (Bernheimer & Jones, 2013, p. 63)

Students in this class understand Mary's frustration. They work in Los Angeles, a city with firsthand knowledge of future trends facing our country and the larger world. It is currently home to people from more than 140 countries who speak 224 languages (World Population Review, 2015). These staggering statistics provide a glimpse into the scope of diversity and change taking place in our society.

Whether we are looking at the increasing ethnic diversity of our population, the annual mobility of 36 million people, the growing number of single-parent families, the increasing number of immigrants and refugees, or the effects of the majority of mothers entering the workforce, families are dealing with an unprecedented rate of change. (U.S. Census Bureau, 2012; Cohen, 2014). Along with these changes comes a world of constantly shifting realities that defy fixed models and clear answers. This new reality has uprooted the core of traditional classroom curricula.

For teachers and directors, uncertainty has not been a positive experience. They enter the profession with a vast store of knowledge and guidelines that they are expected to implement in their work. The uncertainty feels threatening to their professional identity as "experts" in their work with children and families. Yet, the uncertainty of our profession continues to increase along with the world's shifting demographics.

Entering the Unknown

Shulman (2005) writes about the unspoken dilemma of preparing professionals in a time of pervasive uncertainty. She finds that it is rarely possible to use a set of theories or protocol in performing services. Under such conditions, professionals are often entering situations without clear answers. She suggests a pedagogy that is able to embrace uncertainty. In this way, students are being prepared for the uncertainty they will face professionally. It is this kind of uncertainty that emerges as the class reconvenes for a final discussion on their observations.

Joanne tells everyone about her experience of observing at a well-known progressive preschool. She has a look of bewilderment on her face as she describes how much her perceptions have changed. Watching the teachers and children, she realized how controlling the teachers were under the guise of guidance and how many rules they had for every little move children made. She says, "Everything I used to think was so wonderful, I'm now questioning. I watched teachers sitting right next to children doing art work, constantly saying, "only one drop of glue." She ended by saying, "I'm still not sure what to do, but I know it will be different from what I used to do."

Mary joins the discussion with her own experience of questioning how a child was being treated in the class. A three-year-old Middle Eastern boy would not feed himself. Every day, his food would be served and he just sat and stared at it, waiting for somebody to feed him. They all tried to get this boy to feed himself. The teachers were also upset after talking to the parents, who said that he is always fed by them or his grandparents at home. One day, Mary decided to try another approach. She told the boy that she would help him eat his food. She sat with him during meals, taking turns between feeding him and letting the boy feed himself. She proudly announced, "It worked!"

Jones (2007) describes the importance of this kind of willingness to experiment and make changes as a teacher:

> Teaching is a very complex activity that you won't ever do "right." Not entirely. There will always be things you miss, choices you make wrongly, blank moments in which you have no idea what to do. Logical thinking relies on making and testing hypotheses. In a hypothesis, you say: if this, then that. And then you try it, see if you were right, and think some more. Not just by yourself, but with other people. Even with children. (p. 94)

In a field where teachers are expected to be the experts, it can feel unsafe to question their own professional beliefs. The classroom needs to be a place where students feel safe to practice the possibility of reinterpreting and thus reconstructing their early childhood knowledge and ways of working with children (Brownlee & Berthelsen, 2005).

My goal for this class is not to provide the comfort of answers but rather to prepare them for the challenges they will face as educators. As Piaget found in his research, just as children go through disequilibrium as part of their learning process, so students in this class are facing their own sense of disorientation with new kinds of learning and expanded modes of seeing the world (Ginsburg & Opper, 1988).

Our Critical Challenge

Melissa's story is becoming more common as families struggle with such challenges as death, divorce, unemployment, illness, and relocation to unfamiliar and sometimes unforgiving places. Modern families need a place that can care for their children and a community that can bridge the gap between their private and public lives. They need a new kind of "communication community" that can stretch across space and time, bringing people together across their many differences (Couldry, 2004).

The ability to connect with others across all differences is the critical challenge facing early childhood educators today. This remains a difficult issue for the field. In addition to increasing diversity, dealing with the real human dynamics of peoples' struggles, difficult decisions, hopes, and lost dreams often leaves teachers and directors feeling inadequate. In many cases, learning theories, statistical data, and guidelines result in unrealistic expectations, fixed agendas, and a greater disconnection from the children and parents depending upon them.

The knowledge necessary to prevent this kind of disconnection needs a broad range of learning. Katz (2008) discusses the risks of being overly focused on covering vast amounts of information. She is concerned that a disproportionate focus on topics and skills does not provide the understanding needed to withstand the pressures of complicated real-life experience. Instead, she stresses the importance of making time for mastering dispositions, such as being patient, observant, and open to exploring new ideas.

Students need a learning community where they can develop these dispositions through reflecting upon what they have experienced, listening to others, engaging in open dialogue, and coming to a deeper understanding of educational concepts. Storytelling is the vehicle that moves their learning from knowing an array of theories to the wisdom of understanding the true complexity of living experience.

Finding Our Way

After we have listened to a number of biographical presentations, a student gives a surprising talk to the class. Angelo walks to the front of the room for his presentation. He is 35-years old and from an Italian background. He carefully opens a large pizza box filled with pictures and symbolic pizza slices representing parts of his life. Before beginning his presentation, Angelo looks up and shares that he was only able to create his biographical story because he had been listening to their many stories. When he found that he could place himself in other peoples' stories, he discovered the clarity and direction to tell his own story.

Angelo says that at the beginning of this class he did not feel safe enough to share his "true story." But hearing others made him comfortable enough to say, "This is me." Looking straight into their eyes, he adds:

> At first everyone felt like a stranger with a few cliques. I didn't feel comfortable or safe in the class. Listening to your stories changed everything for me. I stopped feeling like we are all strangers. You are all finding your way—just like me. Listening to your stories I felt more able to not always have the answers. There was no need to make up an answer. I could hear from each story that there is not an end. It is okay to not know and realize we are all growing and developing and don't know the final answers.

Listening to Angelo, I am quietly grateful that he is able to put into words the basis of our new learning. Beneath the wildly diverse stories and experiences students are bringing into class, we are discovering an unanticipated gift. We can see ourselves in everyone's story.

Our stories are teaching us that we do not need to fear a world that looks different, keeps changing, and won't let us comfortably use previous answers. Given the dynamics of modern reality with its quality of improvisation and living in uncertainty, we must learn to build these new kinds of relationships and communities. These are skills that can and must be learned (Bateson, 1994; Baxter Magolda, 2012).

Redefining Community

Could it be that the breakdown of our traditional notions of community based on neighborhoods, cultural beliefs, or family background is a necessary step in finding new ways of making our connections with others? Couldry (2004) believes this is true. He observes that our usual way of defining "community" rests on two concepts: (a) the times and spaces where we live, and (b) our sense (both cognitive and emotional) of commonality. Within such stratifications, people's lives move in parallel paths, often without noticing or establishing interactions with those different from themselves.

Early childhood programs cannot afford the seeming comfort of living within these stratifications. Yet, this dynamic makes its way into our programs, leaving staff bewildered when interactions across vast differences are demanded. Finding ways of going beyond these stratifications and building a new type of "communication community" is a crucial task for educators today (Couldry, 2004).

Our classrooms can become this new kind of community where students can safely work with the many difficult situations, feelings, and unanswered questions that are pummeling all of those standing on the crux of a changing society. Freire (1998) believes this kind of living education is our greatest hope for understanding and addressing the challenges facing humankind. Within an educational practice of engaging with diversity through storytelling, dialogue, and reflection, students are much better prepared for the onslaught of issues that will be facing them throughout their careers.

References

Bateson, M. (1995). *Peripheral visions: Learning along the way.* New York: Harper Perennial.

Baxter Magolda, M. B. (2012). Building learning partnerships. *Change, 44*(1), 32–38.

Bernheimer, S. (2005). Telling our stories: A key to effective teaching. *Exchange Magazine, 162*(March/April), 82–83.

Bernheimer, S., & Jones, E. (2013). The gifts of the stranger. *Young Children, 68*(4), 62–67.

Brownlee, J., & Berthelsen, D. (2006). Personal epistemology and relational pedagogy in early childhood teacher education programs. *Early Years: An International Journal of Research, 2*(1), 17–29.

Cohen, P. (2014). Family diversity is the new normal for American children. *Council on Contemporary Families.* Retrieved September 15, 2014 from https://contemporary families.org/the-new-normal

Couldry, N. (2004). In the place of a common culture, what? *The Review of Education Pedagogy & Cultural Studies, 1* (January-March), 3–22.

Delpit, L. (2006). *Other people's children: Cultural conflict in the classroom.* New York: The New Press.

Derman-Sparks, L., & The ABC Task Force (1989). *Anti-bias curriculum: Tools for empowering young children.* Washington, DC: National Association for the Education of Young Children.

Dominice, P. (2000). *Learning from our lives: Using biographies with adults.* San Francisco: Jossey-Bass.

Freire, P. (1998). Pedagogy of the oppressed: The fear of freedom. In A. Freire & D. Macedo (Eds.). *The Paulo Freire reader* (pp. 45–66). New York: Continuum.

Ginsburg, H., & Opper, S. (1988). *Piaget's theory of intellectual development.* Englewood Cliffs, NJ: Prentice Hall.

Jones, E. (2007). *Teaching adults revisited: Active learning for early childhood educators.* Washington, DC: National Association for the Education of Young Children.

Katz, L. (2008). *Challenges and dilemmas of educating teachers of young children.* http://www.naecte.org/docs/Katz%20Opening%20Address.pdf

McDrury, J., & Alterio, M. (2002). *Learning through storytelling in higher education: Using reflection and experience to improve learning.* Wellington, New Zealand: The Dunmore Press.

Moon, J., & Flower, J. (2008). There is a story to be told...A framework for the conception of story in higher education and professional development. *Nurse Education Today, 28*(2), 232–39.

Palmer, P. (2007). *The courage to teach: Exploring the inner landscape of a teacher's life* (10th ed.). San Francisco: Jossey-Bass.

Shulman, L. (2005). Pedagogies of uncertainty. *Liberal Education, 91*(2). http://www.aacu.org/publications-research/periodicals/pedagogies-uncertainty

U.S. Census Bureau (2012). Census Bureau reports national mover rate increases after a record low in 2011. Retrieved December 10, 2012, from http://www.census.gov/newsroom/releases/archives/mobility_of_the_population/cb12-240.html

World Population Review (2015). Los Angeles population 2015. Retrieved September 10, 2015, from http://worldpopulationreview.com/us-cities/los-angeles-population

Chapter 3

The Reflective Practitioner

Our class is now a third of the way through the semester. Students have been engaged in writing a series of journal assignments that examine course readings and key concepts, and then reflecting upon ways this applies to their lives. Looking over their personal reflections, I find them surprisingly thoughtful and honest. They reveal the particular values, priorities, and circumstances of each student's life. Most important, they are part of an ongoing exploration and deepening awareness of the fundamental beliefs students bring into their work as early childhood educators.

Lorena's reflection describes her background and the ways it has given her the tools and strength she needs to achieve her goals. She writes about her life in Mexico and her subsequent immigrant experience coming to the USA:

> I was part of a middle-class, progressive family. My father teaches at a university. I was raised in a home where girls are equal to boys. We grew up doing the same things as boys. We all had household jobs and were encouraged to study hard and live an adventurous life.

I decided to come to the United States at the age of 25 years. I already had obtained a BA degree in Mexico. As an immigrant, I lived according to what I was taught, to work hard and succeed. I immediately began studying English, and got a visa and resident visa. I worked in a factory in New York during the day, and went to school in the evenings.

Sure it was a shock for me working in a factory, being treated with prejudice, and having many unexpected difficulties, but I was certain of two things: Nothing was going to stop me from succeeding and I would never let my parents know how hard this was, since they did not want me to come to the U.S. Even though I had to start my education over, nothing was going to stop me.

These reflections match my experience of Lorena in class. In her mid-forties, she is a dedicated student, always upbeat and smiling. Her assignments are turned in on time and thoroughly researched. She has shared several times her professional commitment as a director to help the immigrant children and families that are part of her program. The rules of success, which form the basis of her value system, have sustained her through hardship and given her the skills she needs to live a successful life. She wants to pass these same values on to the families that are part of her program.

It is after class one evening that Lorena asks to speak with me. She is clearly disturbed. In the privacy of my office, Lorena reveals another side of her experience as a director. She tells me how angry and hopeless she feels about reaching the parents and improving children's lives.

I don't know what's wrong with them. I try to reach them in every way possible. I studied how children develop, and they need to know what these children need. I want to help the parents and children have healthy and successful lives together. They don't show up for parent conferences or parent education meetings. Most of them have been living here for 10 or 20 years, and still can't speak English. We offer ESL classes. Do they come? No!

They're hopeless! The staff and I just make fun of them now. They don't do anything they should to help their children or themselves. I'm an immigrant. I came here by myself at 25. I know how important it is to learn the language. How can you live someplace and not even know how to ask directions, or talk with your child's teacher? My father always taught me to be responsible for myself. When I came here, the first thing I did was take classes to learn the language. I worked during the day and went to school at night. I wanted to learn everything I could to succeed. What should I do with these families?

Watching Lorena's face, I can see the profound sense of despair hidden behind a mask of anger and frustration. Not only is her approach not working, but she has no place left to turn for answers. Lorena has been a dedicated and hard-working director. She understands the fundamental principles needed to create a successful program for families. She knows developmental goals for children and effective parenting practices. She works tirelessly to support her families. Yet, it isn't working. What is wrong? In despair, she and her staff finally blame the parents in order to explain their apparent failure.

A Bigger Problem Than We Think

Lorena is not alone in discovering that her rules for success are not working. The frustration that she and her staff are experiencing is not uncommon. Students are often shocked to discover that their educational principles and understanding of cultural diversity can become an illusion in their work with children and families. Brookfield (1995) believes that one of the hardest things teachers have to learn is that the sincerity of their intentions does not guarantee the effectiveness of their practice. Given the cultural, psychological, and political complexities that are part of all human relationships, teachers' and directors' best efforts can be counterproductive.

The Bubble

Sociologist Melvin Pollner (1987) offers some helpful insights into the kinds of difficulties that are facing early childhood professionals. He believes we all operate within a kind of "bubble" made up of our beliefs, knowledge, and assumptions that help define what is real and unreal, good and bad. This bubble of beliefs goes beyond intellectual understanding. It is deep-seated and intertwined within our emotional makeup. It helps form the core of our identity, our rules for living, and the basis of how we perceive and interact with the world around us.

The bubble of beliefs extends beyond the individual to fields of study and our current academic paradigm. Textbooks and scholarly research largely reflect the belief that factual information makes up true learning, while emotions are volatile and disruptive forces (Liston & Garrison, 2004). Teacher preparation for early childhood professionals follows this basic model of education, relying on theoretical research and its application.

Missing from this educational approach is the value of students' personal experiences and their attending emotions. Without addressing these issues, the scope of learning remains within a narrow range of cognitive-based information, while students maintain their bubble of beliefs. This often results in students either distorting ideas or learning new concepts while holding onto contradictory beliefs (McDevitt & Ormrod, 2008).

Trapped Inside the Academic Bubble

Education based solely on logic and reason has carried a high cost for teachers and directors. Lorena remembers the early childhood education courses in her beginning years of college. She listened to the theories and envisioned applying them smoothly in a choreographed dance that would create successful futures for countless children. She listened, she memorized, she participated, and she received all A's.

But when she became a director, she discovered that reality was not conforming to the models she had studied. Nor was she aware of how her personal experience and beliefs, that is, her personal biases, were influencing her perceptions. Lorena's traditional education was sadly limited. Other very important dimensions of her growth, including self-awareness, had been left dangerously underdeveloped (Mayes, 2005).

Like many early childhood teachers and directors, Lorena and her staff are painfully discovering that cognitive awareness does not prepare them for the complicated and emotional issues that are part of life in a highly diverse society. In particular, they have been unable to understand and work with the complex challenges facing immigrant populations (Saunders, 2010; Suarez-Orozco & Suarez-Orozco, 2010).

Trapped inside their personal and educational beliefs, they resort to making derogatory comments about this population: "They are all on welfare; they milk the system; they just come here from Mexico to have babies and go back; they don't value education." This lack of emotional connection began with their educational experience, but it was now extending into their professional work. It was leading to the defensive stance of a "frightful hardheartedness and absence of feelings" (Vygotsky, 1997, p. 107).

If early childhood educators are to have the capacity to build and sustain caring relationships, we must prepare them to walk the fine line between professional knowledge and empathetic connection with the "unique" person before them. A critical dimension of this preparation is taking students beyond their bubble of beliefs and instrumental role of implementing a preconceived agenda.

Breaking the Bubble

Our class has been engaged with the topic of stereotyping and its many effects on the lives of children, families, and educators. This evening, the class will focus on "invisibility," one of the painful repercussions of stereotyping. Students have been exploring this concept through their latest journal writing. We will be building upon their reflections to develop a deeper understanding of this issue and how it plays out in people's lives.

One part of the assignment asks students to reflect upon invisibility in their own lives. Students were asked to write about a personal experience of feeling invisible and to recall the incident, the accompanying feelings, and the effect on their lives. They were also asked to apply invisibility to an experience in their work. Lastly, they were asked to write about an experience in which they made another person feel invisible, along with its repercussions. Reviewing their journals, I see that their accounts are remarkably detailed, including the event, their emotions, and the many ways it affected their lives.

My short lecture for tonight's class is designed to create a framework for further discussion. I describe the nature of invisibility and its prevalence in people's lives, giving varied examples. Following my lecture, we are ready to begin our small group work wherein each person talks about an experience of invisibility.

From Abstraction to Personal Story

I watch as group members tentatively begin to share their personal stories of invisibility. Soon their stories become more animated and emotional as they experience the caring response of others in the group. I am shocked by the multitude of ways students have felt invisible in their lives. These include childhood experiences of being unseen in the classroom: Marcia, who was systematically ignored by the teacher in a high-achieving fourth-grade class where she was the only African American child; Suaad, who learned to become invisible to avoid constant classroom punishment in Saudi Arabia because she could not speak Arabic. Feelings of invisibility also emerge within families. Sherry felt unseen when her parents divorced and lost all interest in her as a teenager. Jian felt invisible and shamed because his Chinese family expected him to excel in math, and he had a learning disability that made it difficult to work with numbers.

I also hear stories of teachers feeling invisible through isolation and misunderstanding. Maria tells about a Korean family that enrolled a two-year-old girl in her class. For the first few weeks the parents stayed with the child during the day. When they stopped, the child was sobbing nonstop all day. She tried to work with the parents, coaching them to say things like "I will be back in two hours." Maria tried to learn some Korean words to connect with the child. Nothing was working. The parents sent an email to the supervisor, complaining about her. Without asking questions, the supervisor gave Maria the email and said, "Handle it." When the parents removed the child from the program, Maria's isolation spiraled into a crushing sense of failure.

In other cases, students shared experiences of invisibility that led to leaving their jobs. Mitsuko talks about being a new assistant teacher in an infant/toddler program. She was called "stupid" by another teacher when she tried to potty train a child in accordance with her Japanese history. Filled with embarrassment and shame, Mitsuko no longer wanted to continue working there.

Ron recalls a position he held as an assistant teacher for an infant/ toddler program, a job he thoroughly enjoyed. One day, the lead teacher said she needed to talk with him. She informed him that Mary's father called and said that he does not want you changing his daughter's diapers anymore. How do you feel about that?" Shocked, he answered, "How do I feel? I feel very disrespected. I'm really angry. Changing diapers is an important part of our work with children. Why is it a problem?" She answered, "Well, some families don't feel comfortable with a male changing diapers. I talked with the director and she said that you need to limit your work with this child." Ron tells the group, "I was furious and felt completely invisible as a human being. I decided to quit my job."

I notice Lorena in her group. With little emotion, she briefly tells about feeling invisible when she first came to the United States. She quickly adds that she was able to overcome this obstacle through her dedication to succeed. Although she seems disconnected from her own feelings, Lorena is listening intently as others share their experiences.

Carmen, a Latina woman, talks of being treated abusively because of the racism at her school. Watching Carmen's face, it is clear she is struggling with painful memories as she tells her story. Because her parents were migrant workers, the kids shunned and ridiculed her. Teachers judged her because her mother could not help her in school. Her mother worked two jobs, was not proficient in English, and was fearful of the institutional character of schools. She refused to go to any meetings and interact with teachers. The teachers were angry that her mother appeared uninterested in her child's education. Misunderstood and helpless, Carmen tells of becoming more and more withdrawn.

Listening to Carmen tell her story, Lorena's usual upbeat and smiling expression has changed. As Lorena's face shifts from the bravado of judgment to tears of compassion, I understand the power of the spoken word. Tonight, Carmen is telling her story. Yet, she is not alone. As she speaks, the faces of everyone listening reflect their understanding of her struggles. She is moving students from the abstraction of the written word to a direct connection with the living person before them (Cavarero, 2005).

Growing Together

Lorena is clearly shaken as she hears stories of the very issues that had frustrated her in her work as a director. Lorena's shift is more than intellectual. These stories are reaching into the personal struggles and feelings beneath the surface of actual events. Each story is helping students move beyond their emotional and intellectual bubble.

They are discovering a new level of empathy towards themselves and others. Their dialogue and stories are helping them to speak their own truth and to see and hear the humanity of the other person, regardless of differing values and backgrounds. It is this complex exchange that continuously expands their self-awareness and perception of others (Mezirow, 2003; McDrury & Aleterio, 2002). After listening to each person's story, the groups are asked to select one professional dilemma. They are to discuss it and create guidelines for resolution.

One group is listening intently to Maria as she describes in great detail the failure she felt with the Korean family who left the school. She begins crying as she tells her story. I hear members share their concern. Several people acknowledge Maria's strength in this situation and her dedication in continuing to search for ways to work with the child and parents. Various members of the group begin asking questions: How long has she been a teacher there? How does the director usually communicate with staff members? Have there been other similar situations? Do her colleagues help each other?

The discussion becomes quite animated as they begin reflecting upon similar experiences of their own, along with differing perspectives of how Maria might confront this difficult circumstance. Nobody is backing away from the emotions, the messiness, and the uncertainty of a painful situation with no clear answers. They finally decide to list several possible strategies, knowing there could be unexpected responses from the people involved. Allowing these kinds of real-life issues to surface allows students to look at patterns, contradictions, and inconsistencies. In doing so, they are learning to challenge unrealistic ideologies and generate new strategies for solutions (Clark & Rossiter, 2008).

Students are engaged in the kind of learning that can emerge only when the tumultuous outside world enters our classroom. These types of discussions are supporting students in working with difficult situations and thinking through possible solutions. In this way, they are developing the ability to rely on themselves, rather than turning to programmed answers (Baxter Magolda, 2012).

Shifting Identity and Moral Expansion

The last part of the small group work is to examine the ways that class members have dismissed and judged others, thereby making them invisible. Maria acknowledges that she should have learned more about the Korean culture and reached out for help from other teachers. She can see that her fear and frustration with this child and parents led to subtle forms of anger as she tried to control their actions with inappropriate expectations. Without intending it, she believes she left the parents feeling invisible in their relationship with her. Maria adds that she has a lot of new ideas to work with now.

In another group, Carmen recalls that as a child she learned to close herself off from others. While writing her journal assignment, she remembered a situation when she first became a teacher. A mother kept bringing her son in late, disrupting the whole flow of their day. After asking her several times to be on time, she got angry and threatened to have the child taken out of her class. Later, she found out the mother was taking three buses every morning. Carmen remembers the desperate look on the mother's face when she removed her child from the program. She concludes by saying, "You know, writing about how painful it was to be invisible to other people, I can see how this mother must have felt when I treated her this way."

During these sessions I also hear ways that students are bringing a new perspective into their work with children. Diana is telling about a four-year-old girl, Rosa, whose mother had died. She became very disruptive in class. She also continued to cry at school long after the death of her mother. Teachers went from being sympathetic to finally spending more and more time disciplining her. Diana wanted to find a way to reach out to this child whose pain had become invisible to the teachers.

One day, Diana was sitting outside with this little girl. As they talked, Diana recalled the comforting feeling of a safe environment where people could tell their stories without fear of judgment. Rosa talked again of her mother's death. Diana listened, assuring Rosa how sorry she was. Then she decided to share her own story. When she told her that she had a son that died, the girl looked shocked. Then she asked if she was sad. Diana said that when it first happened, she was very sad, but that eventually she decided it was time to stop crying and find interesting things to do. The girl moved very close to her, listening carefully. She then stayed close to Diana, often holding her hand. She also stopped crying all the time.

Knowing how important stories are for children, Diana realized that the message of books can play a valuable role in helping children. She thought of the book *Runaway Bunny* (Brown, 2006), which tells about a bunny who runs away from his mother, turning himself into different forms to hide. But his mother looks for him, and always finds him. Diana decided to read the book at group time. She dedicated it to Rosa. Diana carefully watched the girl as she read, noting how intently she was listening. After the story, Rosa came up to her and said that now she knows her mother is always with her—sometimes she's a bird, or sunshine.

The kind of mutual exchange taking place in our class penetrates the depths of students' emotional and moral belief systems. It multiplies their perspective and resources for solving problems (McDrury & Aleterio, 2002; Day & Tappan, 1996). They are moving away from the need to lay blame and looking with greater depth to the needs of the person before them (Wood, 2000).

Healing Ourselves and Others

Self-reflection is taking students into realms of inner awareness seldom touched upon in academic settings. This includes examining our values, ideals, feelings, and morals. They are no longer trying to transform the world but are allowing themselves to be transformed (Witherell, 1991). A critical outcome of this learning is the expansion of their self-awareness and capacity to care for others.

The early childhood educator is a therapeutic person within the framework of the developing family. The preschool teacher is often the first professional to be intimately involved with children and their families. Within this context, it makes perfect sense to include a self-reflective dimension in programs for early childhood educators.

Unlike training for therapy, our class is making use of inner exploration as it pertains to our practice as teachers. Part of this process is using reflective exercises and shared stories to bring students to a fuller sense of their own humanity and of their commonality with others. Their stories give "true names" to their experience (Carter & Curtis, 2002; Cranton, 2006). Carmen's story does not label her as a shy and withdrawn child, but as a child trying to protect herself from prejudice and rejection. Maria is no longer a teacher who failed with an ethnically different family, but a teacher attempting to reach a family without the use of language or professional support.

Our self-reflective framework for learning reaches far beyond our classroom. Brownlee and Berthelsen (2005) find that a relational pedagogy, which uses a personally connected form of learning and inner reflection, deeply influences the way teachers interact with children. They find that teachers educated with a more instrumental approach, focusing on achieving pre-set goals, tend to use a dualistic perspective of "right and wrong" in their work with children. In contrast, teachers who had a relational learning experience take into consideration the context of a child's life and use a more constructivist approach to teaching.

Listening to students sharing, I hear how their awareness of invisibility is shifting their perceptions. Lorena is beginning to see beyond her own dualistic beliefs. Her path of development is similar to one most of us have traveled. It is often difficult to gain a new perspective in the midst of grappling with our own challenges and beliefs. We need help from others who are going through similar growth (Cranton, 2006).

From Story to Transformation

Lorena quietly watches me as I read the draft of her biographical story paper. Although it gives an articulate and lengthy description of her life, I am struck by the total absence of emotion. When she asks me what I think of her story, I respond that it is well written and certainly touches upon critical events of her life. I also notice that she doesn't include any feelings. Impatiently, she says, "I wrote exactly what happened to me. I don't remember having any feelings." I ask her if she'd like to review the paper with me.

As we look over the paper, I find myself repeatedly asking, "How did you feel when this happened?" Lorena looks at me with a blank expression and says, "I don't know. It was a long time ago." I suggest that she take it home and reflect upon these experiences and see if she can remember how she felt at the time.

As a dedicated student, Lorena returns to my office several times over the next few weeks. Little by little, she begins to insert feelings into her paper. On her third visit, Lorena sits down and hands me the latest version of her paper. This time, it is filled with emotions: the frustration she felt in Mexico as an adult female raised differently from the norm; the loneliness and terror she experienced trying to find her way alone in New York City; her frustration speaking very little English; the humiliation she faced doing factory work and being treated abusively by her employer.

I look at Lorena after reading her paper. Tears are streaming down her face as she says, "You know what I learned from this paper. I learned that when I immigrated against my parents' wishes, I had to prove that I could make it. I was determined to not go back as a failure, and that nothing was going to stop me from making it in the USA." She adds a key insight, "I decided I could never feel emotions again. If I did,

I might fall apart and I had to just keep going." Openly crying, she says, 'This is the first time I've cried in 20 years."

Lorena's confrontation with her past is part of a transformative process that has been unfolding over the course of the semester. I watched as she began to develop an ability to listen to experiences outside her belief system, made tentative steps as she started to express empathy for others, and, finally, learned how to become part of a caring community of diverse people. An important part of this has been her growing ability to reflect back to painful losses, acknowledge them as part of her life story, and use these experiences to enhance her empathy for others. Lorena is not alone in having a storehouse of unexpressed grief. When students feel safe enough to feel and express these losses, more than healing takes place. They become people who feel more deeply and love others more fully (Kessler, 2004).

Writing her biographical story is giving Lorena an opportunity to go through a learning process that is bringing new meaning to her adulthood. Our stories not only give information, but they act as instruments of transformation. Because they allow us to use our own experience as a basis to move into new ways of perceiving our lives, stories provide a passage into personal growth and change.

The next evening, Lorena stands in front of the room with her corn husk doll. She begins by telling the class about how the doll represents the many changes she has gone through in her life. She wants everyone to understand her whole story. Through her stories, Lorena takes us on a gripping emotional journey. They go from funny stories of childhood adventures, to her unbearable pain and loneliness as an immigrant, to her struggle to find a new identity here, and finally to the satisfaction of achieving her dreams.

At the end, she thanks everybody in class for sharing their own stories. She says, "I understand so many issues now, and what people have gone through in their lives. No book could teach me so much. Each biographical story is a living book for me." Listening to her final statement brought tears to my eyes as her instructor:

Now I know that each of my families has their own story. It completely changed me. Their stories can come alive now in my heart and mind. No way will I ever mistreat anyone. I must understand all the pieces of life. I must understand how I can help.

After our last class, Lorena came to see me one more time. She brought up the day we talked about feeling invisible and making others feel invisible. She said that she recognized her own failing in judging parents when she heard Carmen share her story of feeling invisible. She assured me that neither she nor her staff will ever make fun of parents again. She's still not sure of how things will change, but is sure of one thing, "They will never be the same."

A Greater Story

Ricoeur and Blarney (1995) believe our identity is formed through the never-completed stories we tell others and the discovery that our individual story can never be sealed off from the stories of other people. Our self really cannot exist alone. Our personal stories go beyond our world as separate individuals. They take us into a bigger world, one filled with the drama and insights of culture and history. It is a world I would not have connected to early childhood education without a push from my students. In closing this gap between personal and public worlds, we are discovering a place of common culture among all our differences (Couldry, 2004). It is this ability that will be the basis of creating new communities in our early childhood institutions.

References

Baxter Magolda, M. B. (2012). Building learning partnerships. *Change*, 44(1), 32–38.

Brookfield, S. (1995). *Becoming a critically reflective teacher*. San Francisco: Jossey-Bass.

Brown, M. W. (2006). *The runaway bunny*. New York: HarperCollins.

Brownlee, J., & Berthelsen, D. (2006). Personal epistemology and relational pedagogy in early childhood teacher education programs. *Early Years: An International Journal of Research*, 2(1), 17–29.

Carter, M., & Curtis, D. (2002). *Training teachers: A harvest of theory and practice*. St. Paul, MN: Redleaf Press.

Cavarero, A. (2005). *For more than one voice: Toward a philosophy of vocal expression.* Redwood City, CA: Stanford University Press.

Clark, M. C., & Rossiter, M. (2008). Narrative learning in adult life. *New Directions for Adult and Continuing Education,* (119), 61–70.

Couldry, N. (2004). In the place of a common culture, what? *The Review of Education Pedagogy & Cultural Studies, 1*(January–March), 3–22.

Cranton, P. (2006). *Understanding and promoting transformative learning: A guide for educators of adults.* San Francisco: Jossey-Bass.

Day, J., & Tappan, M. (1996). The narrative approach to moral development: From the epistemic subject to dialogical selves. *Human Development, 29*(2), 67–82.

Kessler, R. (2004). Grief as a gateway to love in teaching. In D. Liston & J. Garrison (Eds.), *Teaching, learning, and loving: Reclaiming passion in educational practice* (pp. 137–52). New York: Routledge.

Liston, D., & Garrison, J. (2004). Introduction. In D. Liston & J. Garrison (Eds.), *Teaching, learning, and loving* (pp. 1–20). New York: RoutledgeFalmer.

Mayes, C. (2005). *Education and Jung: Elements of an archetypal pedagogy.* Lanham, MD: Rowman & Littlefield Education.

McDevitt, M., & Ormrod, J. (2008). Fostering conceptual change about child development in prospective teachers and other college students. *Child Development Perspectives, 2*(2), 85–91.

McDrury, J., & Alterio, M. (2002). *Learning through storytelling in higher education: Using reflection and experience to improve learning.* Wellington, New Zealand: The Dunmore Press.

Mezirow, J. (2003). Transformative learning as discourse. *Journal of Transformative Education, 1*(1), 58–63.

Pittard, M. (2003). Developing identity: The transition from student to teacher. Paper presented at the Annual Meeting of the American Educational Research Association. http://files.eric.ed.gov/fulltext/ED481729.pdf

Pollner, M. (1987). *Mundane reason: Reality in everyday and sociological discourse.* Cambridge: Cambridge University Press.

Ricoeur, P., & Blarney, K. (1995). *Oneself as another.* Chicago: University of Chicago Press.

Saunders, D. (2010). *Arrival city: How the largest migration in history is reshaping our world.* New York: Random House.

Suarez-Orozco, C., & Suarez-Orozco, M. M. (2010). *Learning in a new land: Immigrant students in American society.* Cambridge, MA: Belknap Press.

Vygotsky, L. S. (1997). *Educational psychology.* Boca Raton, FL: St. Lucie Press.

Witherell, C. (1991). The self in narrative: A journey into paradox. In C. Witherell & N. Noddings (Eds.), *Stories lives tell: Narrative and dialogue in education* (pp. 83–95). New York: Teachers College Press.

Wood, Diane (2000). Narrating professional development: Teachers' stories as texts for improving practice. *Anthropology and Education Quarterly, 31*(4), 426–448.

Chapter 4

The Long Reach of Our Stories

Looking at me with an uncertain, penetrating gaze, Juana gathers her courage and makes a request:

> I am graduating this coming weekend. I just want to tell you that the first class I took with you changed my life. I discovered a lost dream I had for making a difference in my community. I know I live far from here, but would you come to visit me? I want you to see my community and my work there.

Juana's invitation opened the door for me to see a community far from the academic world of our classroom. That community first came to life for me through Juana's reflective writing. Now I had the opportunity to experience firsthand the long reach of a student's story.

Leaving the winding mountain road, I turn onto a main artery that leads into the heart of the Central Valley of California. I see open fields extending far into the distance. They are filled with produce—almonds, carrots, citrus fruits, grapes, and tomatoes. Along the way, I watch farm laborers bent over picking crops. As the morning turns to midday, I pass town after town. I can feel the hot sun beating down on my car. I am heading to a small farming community, the home and professional workplace of one of my students.

During this long drive to see a student's cultural heritage, I am thinking about the complicated role early childhood programs play in their communities. Watching Juanita as she progressed in her educational work, I saw how her unique history became a driving force to create a program that reflects deeply held values for this little-known agricultural community. This is a common pattern I have seen among my students as they delve more deeply into their own lives. Today, I am looking forward to seeing firsthand the ways our students and early childhood programs are tied to larger forces of social and political dynamics.

Eventually, I see the turn off for her town. Following directions, I arrive at a small home where Juanita is currently living. She greets me warmly, excited to show me her world and the work she is doing as the director of an early childhood program.

Together we head toward the surrounding agricultural fields. As we pass an encampment of old metallic bungalows, Juanita mentions that this is where her parents lived when they came to California in the late 1950s as part of the Bracero program. They were among the millions of Mexican workers who came to the USA for jobs as farm laborers. Work in the fields has now been replaced by more recent immigrant groups of Latinos. This is a community Juanita knows well. This is her family heritage.

A New Beginning

I first met Juanita in a course I was teaching where I ask students to reflect upon stories from their own growth experiences. As a middle-aged woman returning to school after many years of service to her community, Juanita is part of a large group of nontraditional students now entering institutions of higher education. Today, "nontraditional" college students, including low-income students, English language learners, working students, parents, immigrants, and older students, make up a majority of U.S. college and university undergraduates (Bell, 2012; Choy, 2002).

Among the varied written assignments I give, I ask students to write in-depth responses to prompts like these: Describe a detailed story from your childhood that had a major impact on your development. What happened? How did this affect you? What decisions or beliefs came out of this experience?

The students are writing stories, not academic papers; they're entering memory-based conversations. I respond in marginal notes, with questions, affirmations, and sometimes stories of my own. I ask them for their stories and for their thoughts and feelings about their experiences. In this process I hope they will gain new levels of awareness and insights about their lives.

Like other adults returning to college, Juanita brought with her a complex history and a new dream for her life. Dominice (2000) found that it is common for older students to return to college with a profound desire to fulfill dreams for their lives beyond attaining a degree. Yet these dreams often remain unconscious, even though they can provide their deepest motivation.

For Juanita, this kind of dream was still far from her awareness. In fact, she was going through personal changes and an identity shift as part of returning to college. Juanita did not know how profoundly her autobiographical reflections would change her life. Among new insights was her growing awareness of her own identity:

> I began finding out who I am in this class. Before I started writing about my life, I never thought about what really happened or how it affected me. I was shocked when my instructor and I discussed my writing. She kept encouraging me to reflect more deeply on experiences I had been though in my life. At first the writing was very difficult. It made me begin thinking about what really happened to me. It made a real difference in my life.

Juanita's reflective writing would eventually take her into new realities and directions for her life. But they first brought her back into a world of painful memories.

Divided No More

Through her writing, Juanita began the difficult but valuable process of confronting the life, values, and models that came from her family and social world. She was becoming aware of how her self-concept had been shaped by particular experiences and people from her past. With this awareness, she gained the ability to see herself with multiple identities, at times being the hero of her story and other times the victim. It was this ability to embrace all parts of herself and her life that allowed her to accept the full complexity of her identity (Clark & Rossiter, 2008).

Juanita's writing and sharing as part of our classroom community brought a shift in her perception of life:

> During class sessions in my new college program, much of our learning included sharing stories from our lives. I had never shared stories about my life with anybody. It was scary for me. I was afraid of being judged by others. But, as I watched my instructor and classmates responding to stories with understanding and care, I gained the courage to share my own story. It felt wonderful to have the safety of being heard by others who cared about me.

It is through storytelling that students can honor their personal history and use their lives as a source of learning. For nontraditional students, it enables them to bridge the socioeconomic, social, and cultural gap between academic learning and the reality of their lives (Bernheimer, 2003; Exposito & Bernheimer, 2012).

Reflecting upon and sharing her story gave Juanita the courage she needed to begin questioning previous concepts about herself. As she listened to other people share their stories, Juanita discovered she was not alone in having gone through difficult times in her life. With a new level of self-respect, she gained the strength to give her own interpretation and meaning to her past, one that was more historically accurate (Clark & Rossiter, 2008; McDrury & Alterio, 2002):

> It was during this class that I began to have honest conversations with my mother about my life growing up. I shared with her about my brothers' teasing me and beating me up, and how they threatened me if I told anybody. She was very upset, telling me how she had no choice, but to leave us alone. I was

able to hear my mother and understand her situation while honoring my own experience. Before my writing in this class, I was always feeling afraid and keeping secrets. I now was able to express myself, and honor what I had been through in my life.

Juanita was fulfilling an important task. She was gaining an identity that would allow her to move beyond the limitations of her previous self, which was filled with shame and self-negation.

Juanita's ability to move past these limitations required more than cognitive learning; it needed an emotional transformation. Honoring her emotions allowed her to accept changes, go through uncertainty, and construct a new way of viewing herself (Bernheimer, 2003; Shuck, Albornoz, & Winberg, 2013).

This expanded learning model of an inclusive and caring educational community would become a blueprint for Juanita's dream:

> I came out of this experience feeling a new strength within myself. By going back through my life, I brought many different pieces together. I learned to honor what I had been through and realized that I now had the power to direct and change my future. I wanted to use these new insights to help others.

Freedom from the Past

No longer living inside the ghost of her past, Juanita was free to explore deeper passions, wishes, and dreams. Recognizing the ways that a lack of quality care for children and the silencing of communication affected her life, Juanita's previously unconscious dream began taking shape:

> As I wrote and shared about my life, I realized how important it is for children to have a safe place where they will be cared for. The teachers need to let children know that they can communicate about their lives. When my parents worked in the fields, there was no daycare. And families did not communicate about what was happening with them. If we don't learn from the past, the problems just get repeated.

Juanita knew how she could help families in her community. She began formulating plans for a program that would give children a meaningful education and love of learning; ways for staff to connect with parents; and skills for having open and honest communication. She was developing a dream that she could take back to her community, one that could provide what she needed most as a child—a safe and nurturing place in which to learn and grow.

Juanita's growing commitment to make a difference for others increased as she began healing herself. This is not an unusual pattern behind political and social movements. Palmer (2007) discusses how social movements usually begin when isolated individuals who have suffered from a situation that needs to change decide to live "divided no more." Juanita was now ready to bring back to her community a program that recognized the needs and legacy of the Latino farm worker population.

Reconstructing a New Vision

Although Juanita was born a generation later, her identity was formed as part of Latino farm laborers. Her parents toiled long hours in the fields, struggling to find a life in California. Juanita remembers the pain of growing up in poverty and living in a community that looked down on farm laborers.

Juanita lived according to her prescribed role within the Latino community, marrying and supporting her husband to get an education while raising their three children. As her children grew up, she decided to return to college to study early childhood education. She began working as a teacher after receiving her associate's degree. Juanita's decision to continue college for a bachelor's degree led to conflict and a decision to leave her husband. It also led to a journey with a new vision for her life and work.

As Juanita progressed through her educational studies, she began piecing together a vision for her preschool program. Her vision would create a curriculum that is meaningful and inclusive for the migrant Latino families she is serving. It is this vision that Juanita wants to share with me.

Shifting Roles

Today, Juanita is taking me through her community. She points out historical places where people that were part of the Bracero program could come together for recreation and support. As Juanita guides me into this unknown world, I'm aware that our roles are suddenly shifting. I had been Juanita's guide and leader as her instructor, but we will be shifting roles as she leads me into my own extended growth. She will be my teacher today.

We are bringing to life a critical idea for modern educators working with highly complicated social and community differences. We are using education as a process of mutual and continuous adaptation of teacher/student learning. Although this process usually takes place through our classroom narratives, I am learning to watch for openings to explore realities beyond the classroom walls. Vygotsky (1997) believes this is a critical for dynamic and robust learning. He recommends that a teacher's educational work be closely connected to each student's creative, social, and life's work.

Juanita, like other students, brought with her a world unknown to me: family, community, and history. Hearing her story and visiting her community opened my eyes to seeing an expanded reality of her world. In this same manner, Juanita's own reality began expanding in the classroom as she shared and listened to others' stories. She wanted to extend this valuable process to others in her community:

> Through classroom conversations and sharing our stories, learning became real for me. I was hearing somebody's story. I learned how important it is to listen to others. I took this back with me into the world. Now I really listen to people in my community: family, friends, parents, children, and co-workers.

Learning from History

Juanita takes me over to a park where the community holds its annual Harvest Festival. It is filled with people of all ages. I notice there are both older, well-established Latinos who came several generations earlier mingling with new immigrant Latino families working as farm laborers. There is a festive atmosphere.

Juanita's invitation is helping me become acquainted with this community and gain a glimpse into their history. Perks and Thomson (2006) believe that it is through the history of ordinary people that we can come to understand their upheavals and changes. For early childhood educators, this awareness is a critical piece in their ability to give children needed services and an understanding of the sociopolitical system under which they live.

While sitting at a table eating homemade churros, I listen to Juanita and others talk of their lives growing up in this area. Several women are talking about their work in early childhood programs in the community. One woman says that she works very well with the Latino parents in her program because she knows what it is like to be a farm laborer. She also knows the need for good care for their children. Another woman notes that her ability to speak Spanish helps her connect with the children and parents.

Listening to their conversation, I am no longer the person in authority passing my knowledge on to students. I have become the learner. I am learning of past struggles and current ways that a community is working to bridge the gap between their more well-established immigrant population and their newly arrived, more vulnerable counterparts. Most important, my experience with Juanita is deepening my awareness of the need to listen closely to the stories, experiences, and wisdom of my students.

An Emerging Dream

Juanita is excited to take me over to her center and show me the results of her work. Although the school is closed today, as we walk through the yard and classrooms, her vision is evident everywhere.

As we enter the center, the first thing I see is a large bulletin board with pictures of every child's family. Passing into the yard, there is a large garden made up of plants similar to those in the fields of her community, including tomatoes, corn, strawberries, and lettuce. Juanita explains how the garden provides a bridge for the parents in the program. They help the teachers and children understand how to plant and grow their large garden.

The classroom is made up of different centers. Everywhere I look I see a reflection of the children's lives and culture. The dramatic play area has dress up clothes parents brought from home, cooking utensils are similar to ones families use to cook, and even play food fits the Latino culture. The book area has books in both Spanish and English surrounded by pictures of Latino children and families. This is clearly a place where these children and their parents belong.

From Concept to Action

Juanita describes what it was like when she first introduced these ideas as the director. Putting her vision into action has not been as simple or easy as Juanita initially expected. She had much work to do.

> When I first became a director here, the staff was very unhappy. They gossiped and talked about each other behind their backs, there was a lot of anger, and they seemed filled with resentment. The parents who were living in poverty were afraid to talk to the teachers. Because the teachers were educated, the farm workers felt they were different. And everybody looked at me, the director, as somebody above them, who was the authority.

Juanita wanted to bring to the center the kind of open communication she experienced in her college classrooms. She remembered how healing it was to hear other people's stories as well as sharing her own within a safe community. It also taught her ways to dialogue and resolve differences that came up in group discussions. Most important she learned the value of listening to others.

The first thing Juanita did was to start having weekly meetings to help the staff get to know each other through sharing stories from their lives and ideas as well as what bothered them. Juanita started practicing some key principles of her educational experience.

> I knew that as the director, I needed to be a role model for the staff. I wanted to connect with them in a real way. Otherwise, they wouldn't feel safe to talk

to me. I became very open with them and told them that they could come and talk with me, even if they are angry or disagree with me. I let them know, "If anything is bothering you, come and tell me. Even if I don't like it, I promise that I will carefully consider whatever you say to me."

Juanita's approach provided opportunities for staff to build relationships and helped them negotiate tensions as well as supporting them in deepening their own self-knowledge (Carter & Curtis, 2009).

Juanita had many opportunities to put her ideas into practice. Aside from working with the staff, she wanted to have more open communication with parents. She describes a conflict that came up between a mother and one of her teachers. The mother kept getting angry at the teacher. Every time the teacher reminded her of rules they had, like signing in a child when she dropped him off, the mother became furious. The teacher had tried being nice to her and explaining why she asked her to do something. Nothing worked. The teacher came to Juanita in tears. Juanita called the parent into the office to talk with her.

> The mother was working as a farm laborer. She told me that she didn't trust the teacher to take good care of her son. She told me she did not want her son here, but she had to work all day in the fields. She began crying, saying she wanted to raise her son, and they (we) couldn't understand him: "You're all different from us. You don't know what it's like living like we do."

I saw how helpless, sad, and scared she was leaving her son here every day. I told her how sorry I am that she can't stay home with her son. Then I shared with her from my own life, "I understand how hard this must be. My parents worked out in the fields when I was growing up, and had to leave us at home alone. The teachers and I were all raised in this community. We care about you and your son. We all want to make sure your child is safe and is getting a good start for his education. This is why we are here and got educated so that we can do this work." When we finished talking she told me how much it meant to her that we care about her child and that I understood how she felt.

Juanita was facing her first tests as she entered the "swamp." Stott (1995) uses the idea of the swamp as a metaphor for the kinds of complex and messy problems that teachers and directors must learn to work with when they enter the field. In these types of situations, professionals cannot base their response only on the application of child development knowledge and clear rules. Effective leaders need the capacity to be able to make sense out of the mess.

For Juanita, part of making sense out of this "mess" is accepting that conflicts and problems will keep coming up. These can be dealt with through open, honest communication, which, in the case of the distraught mother, helped her begin to trust Juanita. Building on this trust, Juanita had a vision for creating a curriculum with meaningful connections to her Latino families (Carter & Curtis, 2009).

The Food Project

A key area that Juanita wanted to develop in the curriculum centered on food projects. She remembers being shocked at how the teachers resisted making changes to the curriculum. They liked the material and set up of their classrooms. They were angry that I wanted to change things, like the dramatic play area: "We don't want old fashion kitchen utensils and clothes that parents made."

> I shared with them about why I wanted to make these changes. I told them about how I had felt as a child in school, having parents who were farm laborers and being poor. I felt I didn't belong and my parents were afraid of speaking with the teachers. And how these kinds of changes will help children feel they belong in school and that parents can be part of their children's education.

There was also little interest in Latino-based cooking projects. Even though many of her staff came from Latino farm labor families, she realized they never thought of applying traditional forms of cooking to their curriculum. It seemed like too much work, and used up too much time.

Juanita decided to share with her staff a personal story about the role of cooking traditional Latino food in her life:

> I told them about all the ways that cooking could benefit children, and make families part of the program. I also shared with them about cooking with my family while I was growing up. Every Sunday, we would all line up in the kitchen to make tamales together. My mother laid everything out, and we all had our part to do in preparing them. I remember talking and laughing together while we cooked. It taught me so many things, like taking turns, different amounts of ingredients, sharing stories with relatives, and finally sitting together and eating.

Initially the staff was surprised when they heard Juanita's story, but it opened the way for them to begin telling stories about their own experiences with cooking. The more they shared, the more the atmosphere began to change.

Carter and Curtis (2009) believe this kind of facilitation of stories around a meaningful topic is essential for transformational leadership. As the storyteller, Juanita was taking an active role in creating coherence of her vision and its moral implications. It was providing a purposeful way of scaffolding people's learning about themselves, offering a new context in which they could see their life stories through other eyes and form a partnership in building the vision.

Once the teachers agreed to the new curriculum, its benefits for everyone began multiplying, reaching the children, staff, and parents:

> Cooking is an activity that the families relate to well. We invited parents to be part of it. The staff decided to have pot-luck dinners once a month. Parents brought in their favorite dishes. We were all eating and having fun together. The parents trust the teachers now. And the teachers have parents helping in projects like holiday celebrations. They all use food from the garden for cooking projects. It has many hands-on learning and social development benefits for children. It has brought the staff together. They are helping each other plan new ideas for the center, and they go to workshops together. Another benefit has been that parents are more willing to talk with teachers about their children as well as participating in class activities.

Sullivan (2009) found that this is a common outcome from increasing collaboration with families. Among the many benefits, it increases resources for the program, recognizing that each person holds important information about who the child is and what the child needs.

Continuing Work with Staff

Juanita talked about how different staff relations are now. There is very little turnover; teachers work well together and enjoy creating new projects. In examining the importance of supportive contexts for caregivers, Elliot (2007) found that the atmosphere of a center permeates all levels of children's programs. Given the interconnected nature of caring for children, all levels, from administration to teacher aides, affect the atmosphere. Juanita is successfully applying this idea from her initial experience of what made her feel safe and supported as a student. Consequently, Juanita is having great success in creating a stable and contented staff; however, there are some areas of difficulties that have remained stubbornly resistant to change.

Juanita's greatest challenge has been working with those staff members whose education and personal backgrounds have resulted in patterns of teaching that are antithetical to her philosophy. Although most of the staff have been responsive to greater communication and more open connection to others, there are a few who remain stuck and defensive. She describes one of these teachers:

> I have a member of my staff that got her BA degree at a college that didn't use any dialogue or self-reflection as part of learning. She has this poor attitude about life. Even though she's in her early 30s she's become a bitter person. She's smart, but not emotionally developed. I've talked to her about her attitude. She just answers that she got good grades and knows what she is doing.
>
> As a teacher, she doesn't communicate well with children. She'll call across the room, "Maria, bring me that toy." If the child does not respond, she repeats it louder. If the child still doesn't respond, she just gets louder and louder and angrier and angrier. She complains about the children and parents to other staff members.

Juanita is aware that this teacher is an angry person with unresolved personal issues. Without personal reflective work, emotions that simmer beneath the threshold of awareness can have a powerful impact on how we perceive and react, even though we have no idea they are at work (Cranton, 2006; Goleman, 1994).

Juanita also knows from experience that these attitudes can be changed within an educational environment that is safe, caring, and open for people honestly to share about their lives.

> I know that I had a lot of anger when I started college. But from my writing and listening to others, I became able to understand and talk about my life. Now things from the past may cause some pain, but since I can talk about these things, it never develops into a festering wound.

She recognizes that there is a close connection between a teacher's educational experience and their work with children and parents. Juanita is particularly concerned because of the nature of working with young children and their families. At this age, parents and children are very connected. If teachers don't promote open communication, it sets up a pattern in the family and how parents are towards the child in school.

Final Reflections

Leaving Juanita's farming community, I have much to think about during my long drive home. I am inspired by the ways that Juanita was able to make use of her education in her home community. I could see the importance of understanding her cultural heritage and reaching out to others with similar backgrounds.

My visit was also raising questions about the increasing numbers of students who lack a sense of cultural heritage, who do not belong to a community. I am thinking of stories from my students that tell of traumatic uprooting from home countries, students with multiple identities, students who have lost a sense of belonging. Two such students come to mind as I head towards Los Angeles. I am wondering, "How did they find their way through such upheaval? What kind of identity came out of their trauma? Are there new types of resilience we are not yet aware of? How can their lives add to our knowledge base for preparing early childhood educators?"

References

Bell, S. (2012, March 8). Nontraditional students are the new majority. http://lj.library journal.com/2012/03/opinion/steven-bell/nontraditional-students-are-the-new-majority-from-the-bell-tower

Bernheimer, S. (2003). *New possibilities for early childhood education: Stories from our nontraditional students*. New York: Peter Lang.

Carter, M., & Curtis, D. (2009). *The visionary director: A handbook for dreaming, organizing and improving your center* (2nd ed.). St. Paul, MN: Redleaf Press.

Choy, S. (2002). Nontraditional undergraduates: U.S. Department of Education, National Center for Educational Statistics. http://nces.ed.gov/pubs2002/2002012.pdf

Clark, M. C., & Rossiter, M. (2008). Narrative learning in adult life. *New Directions for Adult and Continuing Education* (119), 61–70.

Cranton, P. (2006). *Understanding and promoting transformative learning: A guide for educators of adults*. San Francisco: Jossey-Bass.

Dominice, P. (2000). *Learning from our lives: Using biographies with adults*. San Francisco: Jossey-Bass.

Elliot, E. (2007). *We're not robots: The voices of daycare providers*. New York: SUNY Press.

Exposito, S., & Bernheimer, S. (2012). Non-traditional students and institutions of higher education: A conceptual framework. *Journal of Early Childhood Teacher Education, 33*, 178–89.

Goleman, D. (1994). *Emotional intelligence: Why it can matter more than IQ*. New York: Bantam Books.

McDrury, J., & Alterio, M. (2002). *Learning through storytelling in higher education: Using reflection and experience to improve learning*. Wellington, New Zealand: The Dunmore Press.

Palmer, P. (2007). *The courage to teach: Exploring the inner landscape of a teacher's life* (10th ed.). San Francisco: Jossey-Bass.

Perks, R., & Thomson, A. (2006). *The oral history reader* (2nd ed.). New York: Routledge.

Shuck, B., Albornoz, C., & Winberg, M. (2013). Emotions and their effect on adult learning: A constructivist perspective. http://digitalcommons.fiu.edu/cgi/viewcontent.cgi?article=1270&context=sferc

Stott, F. (1995). Transformational leadership. In E. Jones (Ed.), *Topics in early childhood* (pp. 18–24). St. Paul, MN: Redleaf Press.

Sullivan, D. (2009). *Learning to lead: Effective leadership skills for teachers of young children* (2nd ed.). St. Paul, MN: Redleaf Press.

Vygotsky, L. S. (1997). *Educational psychology*. Boca Raton, FL: St. Lucie Press.

Chapter 5

Tales of the Future

The Bracero program that brought Juanita's Mexican parents to the USA in the 1950s and its counterpart today are a reflection of vast economic, political, and social upheaval that has been rocking the foundations of our world. Whether it's changing economic systems, political instability, wars, famine, or large-scale migration, families and children are often at the center of these radical changes. Masten (2014) believes that the development of children around the world is being threatened by multiple forms of adversity resulting from these massive social, economic, and political upheavals.

This is a critical issue for early childhood educators. Our programs work with children and families during their most formative years. Yet we have little knowledge about development and the formation of resiliency among children who face serious forms of adversity (Masten, 2014).

Stories of Modern Times

Tommy and Cecilia entered my class like all other students. Nothing stood out as unique about either one. Yet they carried within them stories that offer a lens into development and resilience amidst daily trauma. Their stories speak of uprooted families, people torn away from their country by war, political upheaval, and economic hardship. They are stories that also tell of families, teachers, and administrators unable to understand the complicated issues and hardships Tommy and Cecilia faced growing up with immigrant parents and multiple ethnic identities.

The antecedents leading to challenges Tommy and Cecilia would face started long before their birth. Their families came to the USA for differing reasons, far removed from each other geographically. Each family made hard choices, escaping harsh conditions that prevented a viable future in their home country. These were journeys of immense risk into an uncertain future. For Tommy's family, escape was made quickly due to the effects of war. Cecilia's family came slowly in fragmented pieces, fleeing austere economic conditions that were killing their dreams.

A Rocky Journey to the USA

Tommy was born in Vietnam in 1978. He was the second child to parents of mixed ethnic heritage, Chinese and Vietnamese. Although his father operated a thriving lumber company, the aftermath of the war in Vietnam had put them in great danger. Because this family worked with Americans during the Vietnam War, they were now seen as traitors. The family was being threatened and jailed by the Viet Cong.

In desperation, they planned their escape. Tommy was one and a half years old when he left with his family on their journey to a new land. Taking almost nothing with them, they began their getaway late at night. Tommy's father used his money for bribes to get his extended family out of the country. It was a dangerous exit, in which two of Tommy's uncles were caught and jailed. This was followed by a risky boat trip to Hong Kong, where they had to spend an extended period of time in a Vietnamese refugee camp. Eventually they made their way to the USA and arrived at their new home in south central Los Angeles.

Without money, language skills, jobs, or an understanding of American culture, they moved into a low-income neighborhood. Eleven people lived in a one-bedroom apartment. Their household was filled with tension from the stress of being uprooted, crowded, and poor. The difficulties within their household were matched by their hostile surroundings.

The neighborhood, made up of Hispanic and African American families, let them know they did not belong there. Tommy was four years old when they arrived in their new home. He quickly received a clear message from his neighbors:

> When kids played or had parties, I was never invited to join them. I remember one day standing in the balcony of my apartment looking down at a whole bunch of kids having a party next door. I would just sit there and stare at them.

Having left their home country, community, a flourishing business, and a world they knew, they were now starting over in a new land. As displaced immigrants, life would be very different for Tommy's family.

Crossing Forbidden Lines

Cecilia's Jamaican father and Mexican mother each came to the USA to find a better life. Her father's dream of getting an education and becoming an actor and writer drove him to leave Jamaica for New York at the young age of 14. Eventually he moved to Los Angeles. Cecilia's mother emigrated from Mexico when she was 16-years old, and her grandmother had already left several years earlier, escaping the poverty of their small village. Her mother and uncle made their way to south central Los Angeles to reunite with Cecilia's grandmother.

It was in Los Angeles that Cecilia's parents met and fell in love as young adults. Her father was facing the loss of his dreams of becoming educated and a writer. Her mother was struggling to find work with limited English skills. They married and gave birth some months later to Cecilia. Her parents soon learned the consequences of crossing over forbidden lines of race and culture in 1970s Los Angeles. This was a time of great hostility between African American and Hispanic communities. Her parents were even banished by other family members. It was only after Cecilia's birth that her grandmother finally reconciled with her parents.

Initiation as an Outsider

Tommy and Cecilia were at the forefront of growing up as biracial and bicultural children. In 1980, only 3% of U.S. marriages were interracial (Pew Research Center, 2013). As multiethnic children, they did not know they were living in a community mired in poverty and fear, who sought protection through banding together with their own kind. Their entrance into elementary school introduced them to this world.

Tommy's Shocking Realization

Tommy's school was made up of Korean, Hispanic, and African American children. There were no other Vietnamese or Chinese children. He remembers being taunted by other children:

> They would make fun of me when they would see me, and pretend to speak Chinese making sounds that rhyme to make fun of Chinese. They would make fun of my slanted eyes. I was never included in group activities. They would beat me up during lunch or PE time.

Tommy watched his father's attempts at trying to help him. He remembers his father offering to pay a child to be his friend. He also let the teacher know Tommy was coming home with bruises every day. Nothing changed, and the bullying continued.

Cecilia's New World

The children at Cecilia's school were African American and Hispanic. She started noticing that she looked different: "My hair texture was different, and my mother would braid my hair with ribbons intertwined in it like they did in Mexico." The African American girls decided she was violating their picture of a child they labeled as one of them.

When they saw my mother, they asked if that was my nanny. I said, "No, that is my mom." They started laughing saying, "Really, she doesn't look like your mom. How can that be? You're black. You must be adopted."

Cecilia began feeling embarrassed about her mother: "I never allowed my mom to walk me into the playground. I told her to drop me off, because I didn't want to hear what other children would say."

The teasing continued, becoming so intense that her parents were called in to talk with the principal and teacher. Her father told her, "Just say you are half-Hispanic and half-Jamaican." The teacher said she would "tell the children to stop teasing her." Listening, Cecilia realized there would be no help:

> They really didn't understand. Because I was scared to go to school. I dealt with it by just trying to zone myself out. I'd play with my Barbies and read.

Cecilia was also rejected by the Hispanic children: "The Hispanics said I was too dark. They didn't care about who I was."

Elementary school was teaching Tommy and Cecilia lessons far beyond the classroom curriculum. This was a hostile and dangerous place for them. Rejected by peers and with no protection, they had become outcasts.

Adolescence

Both entered adolescence with new hope for acceptance. They longed to find an identity that would enable them to be accepted by their peers. Instead, they found their lives moving towards increasingly dangerous situations. This period of time would lead to long-lasting consequences for their lives.

Tommy's Fading Hopes

Having achieved high grades and tested as gifted, Tommy was accepted into a magnet junior high school. His time in the magnet school offered a brief respite. Tommy did well academically and found a place of belonging in the drama club. But he clearly remained an outsider to the primarily white population. As he says, "I was still an outsider at the school. But I was welcomed as an outsider."

In high school, things changed for Tommy. He started hanging out with a Philippine Asian crowd that was drinking, smoking, and ditching school. When his father saw that his grades had dropped, he gave Tommy an ultimatum: "Shape up or get out." Tommy decided to leave. He moved in with his aunt, who lived in a community that was predominantly Chinese. Once again, Tommy faced rejection because of his bicultural identity—this time among the Chinese students.

> The new high school was predominately Chinese. To this group of Chinese, I wasn't really Chinese, because I was mixed half Vietnamese and my skin tone is definitely darker than typical Chinese. And my Chinese wasn't fluent enough to hold a conversation. Some looked down on me as though I am inferior because of my Vietnamese blood.

This was Tommy's final attempt to fit in.

> I avoided everybody. I would hang out by myself during lunch. I was a lone rebel who didn't conform to any of it. I decided I didn't care. I felt like, "If you think you're too good for me to hang out with, I'm already used to being out casted from different social groups. This is nothing new."

His stance as a "lone rebel" did not protect him. Asian gang members started beating him up because he refused to join. There was one crack in Tommy's isolation. As a senior, he recognized that some younger boys were also being victimized by gangs. He began to find ways of protecting them: "I became kind of like their big brother. I knew from experience what they were facing, and started providing a safe place for them during vulnerable times, such as lunchtime." Beyond protecting these boys, Tommy had no connection with peers or teachers. With low grades and a defiant attitude, he barely graduated from high school.

Cecilia's Dangerous Search

During junior high school, Cecilia was confident that her identity was Hispanic. Unfortunately, this would backfire for her. The African American girls turned against her, beating her up outside the school and following her home. School officials suspended the girls, but nothing further was done to solve the problem. Cecilia tried turning to her parents for help:

> It was like it went totally over their heads. They just thought I was having my typical teenage tantrums. But I was trying to let them know my feelings. They would tell me certain Bible verses. And to pray. But that's not going to help me when the girls physically harm me.

Her parents' ineffective communication when faced with these problematic situations is common among immigrant parents (Nesteruk & Marks, 2011). Eventually, Cecilia found temporary relief by changing to a different junior high school.

In high school, the African American girls resumed their attack. They started rumors about Cecilia. One rumor said her mother was raped by a black man. Another rumor said she was adopted. Students began laughing at her and teasing her:

> I became more timid and shy. I even started stuttering. It affected my self-esteem. In the classroom, I wouldn't raise my hand. I didn't want to draw attention to myself.

The school did nothing. Once again, Cecilia was left to find her own way to survive.

Tommy and Cecilia, like other adolescents, searched for an identity that would allow them to have companionship and acceptance. This did not happen. Instead, their identity as outcasts became solidified throughout their years in high school.

Connected Stories

Tommy and Cecilia were dropped into a world totally different from their parents' place of origin. As biracial children, their experiences of agonizing pain and rejection mirrored each other. They also shared a common need of all children to be accepted and find a place for themselves as part of their family, school, and community.

In the end, Tommy's and Cecilia's stories are typical of many children who came to abandon hope of finding a place for themselves in their school and community. Their formative years of adolescence brought a renewed search for belonging, ending in a final despairing break in their struggle for acceptance. Whether it took the form of Cecilia's withdrawal inside a shell of self-protection or Tommy's lashing out as a lone rebel, their time in our school system ended in hopeless despair.

Changing Direction

Tommy's Rocky Start

After graduating from high school, Tommy started taking courses at a community college. And he continued his relationship with the young high school boys whom he had befriended. However, during his first semester he found himself confronting violence again. While visiting them, one of the boys was attacked by gang members: "I tried to get in there and help him. We were forced to fight back." Assault charges followed. Tommy was now 18 years old.

Following this occurrence, Tommy dropped out of college and started working. It would take another 15 years before he returned to school. A key experience during this time was his sister giving birth to twin girls. Tommy was intrigued watching their growth. This new interest planted a seed of motivation and purpose. After many years of scattered jobs and an unsettled life, he decided to return to college to study early childhood education.

Cecilia's Discovery

Following high school, Cecilia attended a state university where she had her first breakthrough in understanding her identity. She joined an extracurricular multicultural group, where she felt safe to begin exploring her identity. One of her favorite psychology professors coined a term, "Jamexican," which she still uses to describe herself. She was excited to discover this identity and completed two years at the university. She then went on to work as an early childhood teacher for the next ten years.

A New Journey

In their mid-thirties, Tommy and Cecilia decided to continue their college education. They both brought with them a deep commitment to move forward with their lives, and the maturity to do the necessary work to achieve their goals. They also brought emotional scars from a lifetime of social rejection.

Tommy's Awakening

Walking into the classroom, Tommy looked like a picture of the all-American boy. He wore jeans, a T-shirt, and a baseball cap reversed. Smiling and friendly, he seemed happy to be in the class. He was enrolled in two courses with me: one focusing on understanding children and parents, the other examining literacy development. During our introductions, he expressed his enthusiasm to be at the college and his commitment to work hard and finish his degree.

Although Tommy had been through many experiences, one thing he had never done was to think about his past. His reflective assignments initiated a new course of self-discovery. Tommy recalls how self-reflective assignments in two courses simultaneously led to profound insights about his life. His first breakthrough came from writing a timeline and description of events covering experiences in his life.

He describes how his first timeline assignment opened up a forgotten period:

> My insights started with writing a timeline for your class. You gave me feedback that it was a very short timeline. You said, "There must be something else. Think about it."

As Tommy reflected upon his timeline and biographical story assignment for another class, he began to remember a forgotten time in his childhood. These assignments brought back how difficult it was for his immigrant family. His mother was 1 of 13 siblings: "And she came here without any of them." In addition, he recalled his mother's conflicts with her mother-in-law and the inevitable isolation and depression that followed. It also brought back hidden memories of his father's long hours at work and his anger when he returned home.

Tommy's new awareness began the awakening of his true story. It was in remembering these events that he began to understand his childhood, including ways that he blocked painful memories of his immigrant family. Suarez-Orozco and Suarez-Orozco (2002) discuss how immigration is one of the most stressful events a family can go through, taking away their significant relationships, including extended family, friends, and community.

Tommy's continuing reflections also brought back intense emotions. He started realizing the extent of alienation he felt at home and school while growing up. His father's abusiveness, the cruelty of classmates, the beatings and other dangers in his neighborhood that made him intensely angry: "I was full of hatred and bitterness in myself when I was growing up. I was just always, always angry." Recognizing the degree of his despair and anger was a necessary part of seeing a more complete picture of himself (Kessler, 2004; Shuck, Albornoz, & Winberg, 2013).

Cecilia's Recollection

Cecilia presented a very different picture from Tommy. She walked into my communication class with a serious look on her face. She was dressed in a conservative-looking sweater and skirt. Beyond their differences in appearance and manner, both were dedicated to completing their degree.

Cecilia's journal writing brought a new awareness about how much her experiences had affected her view of herself and the world. She started describing her self-observations during our weekly class sharing:

> I was very insecure. When I communicated with others, I was very abrasive, always defending myself. Also, I was judgmental. I had certain views on different cultures, like stereotypes. It was a constant battle. I was very defensive in my talking.
>
> Because of what happened to me in my background, I would always think somebody had an ulterior motive. Or that they already had a perception of me. I was a girl. And my height. And the fact that I'm mixed. And that I may come off like I'm better than them.

Cecilia was also becoming aware of her parents' struggles as immigrants and as a multiracial couple. She recalled their crushed dreams, her bus driver father's aspirations to be a screen writer, her mother's struggles with English and her limited work opportunities. She remembered their arguments about finances and how to raise children: "They had troubles as a multiracial couple. They didn't have like a partnership."

Tommy and Cecilia's emerging stories opened the door to unconscious patterns of beliefs about themselves and others. Awareness of these beliefs is a critical part of the journey of personal transformation (Cranton, 2006). Fortified with these revelations they took their first steps towards self-awareness and exploring possible identities for their lives. Their ability to safely reflect upon these experiences within a supportive classroom community along with encouraging feedback from the instructor opened the door to a new view of themselves and others.

New Realities Emerge

Tommy and Cecilia started moving beyond the constraints of their distrustful views of the world. They began to listen to others and explore other possibilities from which they previously felt excluded. Tommy started rethinking his past experience:

> I was able to analyze it in retrospect. To give reason to my past. To understand why I was angry. To realize that I did have choices that I didn't consider back then. Up until that time I justified my anger from when I was growing up, but I never analyzed it. It was more like, I was being a tough guy, because I didn't want people to pick on me. I was isolating because I didn't want to be teased. It wasn't until I began analyzing why I was being laughed at, why I was being teased—that's when I fully comprehended the whole situation.

As Tommy continued his reflections, he gradually lost the need to defend himself. In his words, he had learned how to "agree to disagree" and to say, "I understand your side." And as he reflected on his home, he learned forgiveness: "I became more compassionate to my mom's experiences. And my dad as well." This new perspective allowed him to move beyond past labels and gave him a new sense of worth.

Cecilia's growing self-awareness through class reflections, journal writing, and discussions began opening new ways of perceiving herself:

> There was an exercise where you had to fully listen to someone. The first time around I was thinking of stuff and not really listening. You asked us what were we thinking and feeling while the person talked. You made us aware. The second time around you asked us to really listen to the person without thinking of what you were going to tell them. That was like "Wow!" Before I was really just trying to figure out what I was going to say to the person.

Tommy's and Cecilia's journeys into expanding their realities meant leaving their past perceptions and beliefs behind. Such a shift involved more than cognitive transformation. It included the need for an emotional transformation as they faced the fears and uncertainty of a new reality (Shuck et al., 2013).

Double-edged Sword of Growth

Neither Tommy nor Cecilia anticipated the changes this would bring to their lives. They assumed that their new learning and achievements would be welcomed by family and close friends. Instead, their relationships with key people in their lives became increasingly strained.

Tommy's Unanticipated Consequences

It was during Tommy's biographical story presentation that he first alluded to feelings of isolation with his return to college. Tommy's greatest disappointment was with his family, who valued business as a path to success:

> None of my family members truly cheered me going through college. I didn't feel their support. I could hear them say, "Good for you. Good work." But I didn't hear any genuine support when I was telling them that I am halfway through this, or I have one degree down.

By contrast, he expressed gratitude for classmates who had become his new family, who understood and accepted him exactly as he was: "I am unique, very self-analytical, a bit obsessive compulsive."

His deepest grief came with his graduation: "Mom couldn't take a day off work. No one came, because it fell on a Saturday. We had a dinner but it didn't feel like a celebration to me." He remembered how he felt. "It hurt a lot."

Cecilia's Unexpected Repercussions

As Cecilia continued her education, she began seeing cracks in the foundation of her life. Her boyfriend of 14 years accused her of being "fake" when she remained calm during a disagreement. He called her "Miss Professor," and let her know, "This is not going to last."

While Cecilia was trying to deal with this new threat to her relationship, she realized that the changes within her were also disrupting her ties with her family.

> It's almost like I'm the Black Sheep of the family. I'm not included in their planning. Like they all got together a few days ago. My sister told me, "We were going to call you, but you were probably at some school event." It's the cost. Going to school and becoming empowered and how to work with society. And in personal relationships.

With the painful alienation she was feeling with her family, Cecilia shared how important it has been for her to hear other students' stories:

> I noticed a theme of student sharing about having difficulties with their family members or being rejected. It was helpful to hear those stories, because I related to it and we talked about it and came up with solutions. It made it much more rich, just hearing that feedback and encouragement.

Expanded Identity

Through ongoing personal reflection, sharing their stories, and listening to others, Tommy and Cecilia were gaining a narrative identity as they connected the events of their lives, along with its healing effects on their suffering. They were able to acquire a new perspective on their lives, learning lessons and gaining insights about how they came to be who they are today (McAdams & McLean, 2013). Each developed a new understanding of themselves, including a realization that all of us are affected by a lack of support. Motivated by an expanding desire to help others facing similar adversity, both decided to work towards a Master's degree.

Tommy's New Path

While taking classes, Tommy started working in three programs to help young people in need. He was working at outreach programs serving high-risk high school and college students; as a mentor for early childhood teachers; and volunteering as a college advisor at a youth center that provided services for low-income students. He describes it as giving back to others what he had needed as a child. And now he wants to take his work a step further, to make a bigger impact: "I want to pursue a Master's degree."

Cecilia's Expanded Vision

Cecilia has also decided to obtain a Master's degree and become a therapist. She describes her reason for this new goal:

What I want to do in our society with my education is to become a marriage and family therapist in order to empower young adolescents and teens whose lives have been interrupted by violence, bullying, abuse, poverty and other traumas by giving them the necessary tools and guidance to overcome their challenges and attain their goals. Because the majority of youth don't have positive role models in their life.

I think my life experiences will help me in my career because I will be able to relate and have authentic compassion to most of the sensitive and critical issues that the majority of teens are faced with in their daily lives such as bullying, growing up biracial, living in a dysfunctional home where your voice isn't heard and feelings aren't validated.

With their new purpose to serve others who have been through similar traumas, Tommy and Cecilia will be coming full circle from their lives as victimized children to empowered professionals committed to helping others

A Paradigm for the Future

Historically, to be like the majority has been a major predictor of success in the American educational system. Most efforts to support the education of minority students in all categories have seen "catching up" with standard norms as the only option. It is an educational paradigm based on rational and intellectual learning, and one that suppresses the emotional and interpersonal dimension of development. Within such a system, we lose sight of the full humanity of students and teachers (Argyris, 1974; Dale, 2004).

In contrast, a relational and transformative approach to education advocates for honoring diversity. It acknowledges all the challenges of being different, but it is able to transform those challenges from weaknesses to sources of strength through insight and courageous innovation (Argyris, 1974; Dale, 2004).

New Forms of Resilience

Tommy's and Cecilia's unfolding stories taught me how resilience can take on forms I never before considered. Masten (2014) defines resilience

as "the capacity of a dynamic system to adapt successfully to distur-
bances that threaten system function, viability, or development" (p. 6).
Tommy's and Cecilia's repeated attempts at "trying to find a way to fit
in" were clearly forms of persistence and efforts to adapt to the social
structure. A less obvious form of resilience was their final despairing
realization in high school that nothing they did was going to work.
Tommy's decision to retreat into an armored facade as a lone rebel and
Cecilia's withdrawal into a reserved mask were effective ways of protecting themselves from a hostile and dangerous environment.

Following their time within the constraints of educational institutions and dependency on family, they began exploring new possibilities for their lives. It was over an extended period that each began a
developmental journey that remained hidden for many years. I learned
from their stories that during this time, which appeared to be chaotic,
static, or regressive, each was developing clarity about their priorities,
new strengths, and the seeds of a passionate purpose for their future.

Reflective storytelling as part of their education moved Tommy and
Cecilia further along their new paths. Their stories provided the vehicle
for understanding their own lives. Sharing their stories and listening to
others expanded their perceptions of others (Bernheimer & Jones, 2013;
McDrury & Alterio, 2002). This process of transformational learning
was not an easy one for either of them. The journey often included
times of grief and pain as they confronted and let go of an old way
of living (Cranton, 2006). Yet, in going through this process they were
creating a new foundation upon which their resilience could continue
to grow.

Conclusion

The vast increase of population movement and intermixing of races
and cultures are two of the most prevalent trends of our time. Tommy's and Cecilia's stories graphically illustrate the heartbreaking consequences of growing up at the cutting edge of these future trends. It
is a world filled with the struggles of children living as outcasts within

their family, community, and school, all lacking the ability to understand or truly help them.

Yet, both found forms of resilience that were able to emerge in adulthood, allowing them to move towards a new purpose and further education. The unfolding process of their development into productive, insightful, and contributing adults raises hope that an informed and innovative educational model can address these multicultural challenges and prepare self-aware, compassionate, and effective childhood educators.

References

Argyris, C. (1974). Alternative schools: A behavioral analysis. *Harvard Educational Review, 41*(4), 550–67.

Bernheimer, S., & Jones, E. (2013). The gifts of the stranger. *Young Children, 68(4),* 62–67.

Cranton, P. (2006). *Understanding and promoting transformative learning: A guide for educators of adults.* San Francisco: Jossey-Bass.

Dale, M. (2004). Tales in and out of school. In D. Liston & J. Garrison (Eds.), *Teaching, learning, and loving: Reclaiming passion in educational practice* (pp. 65–84). New York: RoutledgeFalmer.

Kessler, R. (2004). Grief as a gateway to love in teaching. In D. Liston & J. Garrison (Eds.), *Teaching, learning, and loving: Reclaiming passion in educational practice* (pp. 137–52). New York: RoutledgeFalmer.

Masten, A. (2014). Global perspectives on resilience in children and youth. *Child Development, 85*(1), 6–20.

McAdams, D. P., & McLean, K. C. (2013). Narrative identity. *Current Directions in Psychological Science, 22*(3), 233–38. Doi:10.1177/0963721413475622.

McDrury, J., & Alterio, M. (2002). *Learning through storytelling in higher education: Using reflection and experience to improve learning.* Wellington, New Zealand: The Dunmore Press.

Nesteruk, O., & Marks, L. D. (2011). Parenting in immigration: Experiences of mothers and fathers from Eastern Europe raising children in the United States. *Journal of Comparative Family Studies, 42*(6), 809–25.

Pew Research Center (2013). Intermarriage on the rise in the U.S. http://pewresearch.org/…/intermarriage-on-the-rise

Shuck, B., Albornoz, C., & Winberg, M. (2013). Emotions and their effect on adult learning: A constructivist perspective. http://digitalcommons.fiu.edu/cgi/viewcontent.cgi?article=1270&context=sferc

Suarez-Orozco, C., & Suarez-Orozco, M. M. (2002). *Children of immigration.* Cambridge, MA: Harvard University Press.

Chapter 6

Paths to Leadership

Today, Tommy and Cecilia are both engaged in graduate studies, which hold the promise of realizing their dreams of making an important contribution to our society. Lei and Jenny, the two women in this chapter, take us further along the path to understanding how leadership can emerge from unlikely places and backgrounds.

Sullivan (2009) believes that becoming a leader is a developmental process that demands creating and interpreting your own life experiences and knowledge. Like human development, the process of becoming a leader takes time and is never finished. Lei and Jenny's stories show the ways that unexpected twists and turns in their lives brought them to new paths, new perceptions, and leadership roles in early childhood education.

Lei's story is an international saga beginning in Taiwan and ending in Los Angeles. Jenny's story reveals a journey within her native country of New Zealand, yet one that took her beyond the confines of traditional goals. Both women experienced painful encounters growing up, limitations of gender and cultural expectations, and the restrictions of traditional educational practice.

They were eventually able to rise above these life experiences and apply their insights to create new models that infuse life into the classroom and respect for each learner. Together, they represent a template of how our personal paths can join with professional commitment, transforming our approach to teacher preparation.

A Journey across International Borders

Lei never expected to be living in the Los Angeles area. Nor did she imagine that she would be doing groundbreaking work in teacher preparation with Chinese immigrant home daycare providers. When I asked what led her to this work, Lei said simply, "My life. I have an understanding of their position and how they are limited or trapped in their lives."

A Painful Beginning

Lei was born and raised in Taiwan as part of a middle-class family that had left an urban center in southern China. Lei's challenges began at birth. Born as the second daughter to parents who desperately wanted a son, her birth was a great disappointment to her family.

Not only was Lei a female, but she was born with a twisted arm. In a culture that considers it shameful to have a child with a defect, Lei was discriminated against everywhere, including within her family.

> At home, nobody said anything, but you could tell that they felt I would never become anybody important. They gave me the message, "She can't do anything. She's no good."

The next year her brother was born. Her baby brother became the treasure of the family. Lei's father put all his dreams and hopes on her brother to carry the name and honor the family.

Growing up, Lei describes herself as "not happy." She learned to quietly live within a world where she was viewed with shame and discrimination. Her first break with these limitations was to surprise her parents by getting into college in a home economics program. They still let her know, "If you are lucky you will find a good husband and be set."

An unexpected family crisis would forever change the direction of Lei's life. Their family was notified that her brother had died in army training camp. Her father was devastated. All his dreams and hopes that her brother would carry on the family name were crushed. Even amidst this tragedy, Lei remembers:

> Nobody talked about their loss, just as they had never discussed the repercussions of my disability. I just wanted to get away from all the unspoken pain with my family.

The opportunity soon presented itself. Her father offered the money he had saved for his son's education to Lei's older sister, who refused it. When the money was offered to Lei, she immediately accepted: "With all the disappointment with my family and the memory of my brother, I couldn't wait to leave and come to the USA." By age 20, Lei had completed her bachelor's degree in home economics, passed the English exam, and was accepted at a U.S. university. With hopes for a new life, Lei ventured off to the United States.

A Journey within Her Homeland

Far from the world of Taiwan and Los Angeles, Jenny was taking her own journey toward the field of early childhood education. Born and raised in New Zealand as part of a white family, Jenny never faced the challenges of a physical disability or difficulties as an ethnic/immigrant. Yet she experienced other ways of being marginalized and constrained while growing up.

A Limited World

Jenny grew up following the prescribed way of living in her 1950s working-class community in New Zealand. She stayed within the expected path for a female through high school, eventually deciding to become a secretary. Jenny describes the views of women in this conservative community:

> Women work until they get married and then stay home to care for husbands and children. I have no recollection of there being any real importance placed on education, and my mother would have been quite happy for me to leave school as soon as I was old enough.

The death of Jenny's father when she was five years old quickly put her family outside the acceptable standards. Growing up in a marginalized single-parent family, Jenny lived with a sense of isolation from the rest of the community. Her feelings of isolation deepened as her mother became ill. She now had to play quietly by herself at home, rarely having friends over. Living inside this lonely world, Jenny remembers thinking, "There must be something better than this."

Glimpse of Light

Jenny's first glimpse into another world came when her school got a library:

> I think I was 7 at the time and I discovered real BOOKS! Library books were to become my "at home" friends, something that was acceptable—they didn't make a noise, nor did they make a mess, nor did they cost anything.

Her books began quietly introducing Jenny to an exciting world beyond her community.

Another ray of light was spending time living with her aunt's family because of her mother's illness. Her aunt's home showed her a life "very different from my quiet, tidy home environment. My aunt was always positive and believed that any challenge could be overcome. She became my role model." Jenny thought, "I want to embrace life in the same way."

Jenny's turning point came unexpectedly with her entrance into secretarial school. She knew right away it was a mistake. For Jenny, saying "no" to this expected path for women was the beginning of choosing a new life. She now wanted "a career that would truly interest me."

She decided to attend college and study home economics. Her studies led her to new professional opportunities, beginning with becoming a high school teacher. During the 1970s, Jenny's life matched the changes taking place for many women in an "era of great societal change." Unlike her mother and extended family, she had been to college and launched a professional career. Jenny had broken away from generations of past women.

Yet, she was teaching home economics, whose class textbook had a photo on the back cover of a bride running towards the camera: "I felt that I was living a somewhat 'patchwork life'—supposedly educating aspiring brides." But Jenny had other ideas. She wanted to open her students' eyes to see that there is a wider world of possibilities for their lives.

A Bigger World

With the completion of their bachelor's degrees, Lei and Jenny's worlds were about to take a leap forward. As the opportunity presented itself, they were ready to step out of their past and into the future. This ability to leave the constraints of their tribal group behind was found to be a key trait in adults living fulfilling lives and making a significant contribution to others (Daloz, Keen, Keen, & Parks, 1996). Lei and Jenny were now free to explore new possibilities for their lives. Neither woman knew the kinds of challenges and risks each would be facing on this new journey.

Entering an Alien Reality

Lei describes her experience of coming to the USA:

> I arrived alone with two suitcases and was quickly thrown into a world I did not understand. American culture was confusing, and I could barely speak English. Even the emotional neglect I felt in my family did not prepare me for this experience of total isolation.

Without friends, family, or community, Lei began her struggle to achieve the education that would be the key to a new identity: "I remember sitting in the back of the classroom feeling like an idiot. I was studying

twenty hours a day, and using a dictionary to translate every textbook."
Lei continues:

> I went through my entire master's degree program in educational psychol-
> ogy without ever saying one word. There was no storytelling. Everything was
> data and research.

Her hard work and persistence paid off. Eventually Lei completed a
Master's degree, married, and moved to Los Angeles. It was in Los
Angeles that Lei began her career in early childhood education.

> At her first job in an early childhood program Lei worked very hard. She
> wanted to make use of her hard-earned education. She soon came up against
> an unexpected barrier— organizational bias. Lei realized, "Only white people
> get into management or receive the correct pay. When I brought this up with
> a member of the board, I was let go from my position." Lei's response to con-
> fronting this institutional bias was anger. She decided to return to college. She
> wanted to pursue her doctorate with a clear goal in mind: "to address social
> injustice and cultural diversity."

Jenny's Entrance into Early Childhood

After teaching high school for a number of years, Jenny's own world
was about to get larger. She was asked to be part of developing New
Zealand's first college-level nanny program. She soon realized the con-
troversial nature of educating students to work with young children.
The program was attacked from both sides of the political spectrum.
Jenny discovered that educational programs preparing students to care
for young children had many adversaries. These included those who
rejected the idea entirely, as stated in her local newspaper:

> Motherhood is a career in itself and a woman should decide before bearing
> children what career she wishes to follow. There can be little satisfaction or
> fulfillment in bearing children and then handing them over to a nanny for
> most of their waking hours. (Anonymous, 1984)

Other critics came from the feminist movement who felt that bright
girls should study in elite, male-dominated professions, such as law,

medicine, and engineering, rather than fields that care for young children. This denigration from both sides deepened Jenny's commitment to show that this was an important and legitimate field of study. She wanted to develop a quality program with strong roots in early childhood. As part of this new dream, Jenny decided to get a Master's degree in early childhood education.

Education and Empowerment

Lei's and Jenny's first steps into a bigger world brought them face-to-face with institutional bias and oppression. Unlike their childhood, which left them few options in the face of oppression, both women now responded by taking action. They decided to return to college. Just as today, increasing numbers of women are taking a similar journey. Currently in the USA, a radical shift in attendance has more women than men attending college (Gonzalez, 2012). For both women, education would be the key to attaining a more powerful identity.

Lei's New Awareness

As part of her doctoral program, Lei took a narrative research class. This class would be a life-changing experience for her, both personally and professionally: "In writing my life story, I brought all the pieces together." Life began to make sense for Lei. She understood how her life had been affected by cultural and familial beliefs. For the first time, she could see beyond the personal shame and pain she had lived with while growing up. She now knew that she could rise above the constraints of her early years.

Lei also realized a larger benefit from personal reflection and sharing:

> Listening to other students share their stories, even from different cultural and racial backgrounds, deepened the insights I was gaining about myself. The sense of isolation I experienced as an immigrant lessened as I heard the struggles and triumphs of other people's lives.

This experience planted the seed of storytelling as a way to infuse new life in classroom learning.

Jenny's Unexpected Insight

While studying for her master's degree in early childhood education, one assignment brought a new awareness to Jenny's life. She was asked to write about the nature of New Zealand society using Bronfenbrenner's ecological model. Bronfenbrenner's ecological theory (Paquette & Ryan, 2000) examines multiple spheres of influence on a child's development, including the child's perception of these influences.

As she wrote, Jenny was able to understand how her own life was affected by complex forces beyond her personal interactions, including the historical time in which she was raised in New Zealand. This was her first experience of the importance of self-understanding as part of education.

Lei's and Jenny's new awareness from their life reflections would be an important factor in their paths towards leadership. This self-examination enabled them to reconstruct their past and imagine a future with a greater sense of unity, purpose, and meaning (McAdams & McLean, 2013). With their new level of education and greater sense of identity, they were ready to move into leadership roles.

Initiation into Leadership

Positions of authority began opening for Lei and Jenny. Initially, both held traditional views of leadership as being at the top of a hierarchical structure (Preskill & Brookfield, 2009). They saw their instructor role as one of helping students gain insights they, as "experts," regarded as valuable. Embedded within this view was their assumption that they knew best what insights were important and how their students should think about them (Baxter Magolda, 2012). Their upcoming experiences would force them to rethink how they viewed themselves, their leadership, and their roles as instructors.

Lei's New Direction

Lei was teaching a parenting class while attending the doctoral program. She began teaching them with prepared lectures on a variety of topics. Each week, she noticed the parents showed little interest in her lectures. Remembering her experience in the narrative research class, she decided to try something different:

> I knew the value of storytelling, so I decided to use my own story as part of explaining the concepts I was teaching. The parents immediately responded. They began sharing the struggles of feeling helpless with an out-of-control child, an abusive husband, or the confusion of raising a child in a strange new world.

Becoming a community college instructor would further change Lei's previous beliefs about leadership and teaching. Lei saw injustice once again. She watched the largely minority population of students going through classes, disconnected from the material, but receiving passing grades. These painful observations brought back her own memories of being invisible and silent as a college student after coming to the USA.

Lei decided to try using storytelling in the college classroom. She knew it meant undoing all her previous beliefs about being an instructor. She also knew this was a way she could address the injustice she saw at the college. She began asking students to share personal stories related to topics they were covering.

She immediately saw a new dynamic forming among the students. When they began sharing their stories, they realized there were others who had also been through hard times, they were not alone. With this recognition, they began working together as a group. Lei also saw that it was helping them emotionally as they began appreciating their own lives and what they had been through. Most striking was seeing a new excitement in their involvement with learning as it took on new meaning. Lei had started a new path as an instructor, one that would lead to further work towards social justice.

Jenny's New Search

By the 1990s, Jenny had developed a recognized early childhood teacher education program. She was thoroughly prepared for her new role as a college instructor. Jenny entered the classroom with well-organized, clear, and concise lectures, along with related assignments. Each assignment gave detailed directions for applying this information. When reading them, she carefully pointed out errors that needed correction.

As the semester progressed, Jenny was shocked to see that her carefully planned assignments were leaving students feeling confused and unsure of their work. When they asked for more clarification, Jenny further discussed all the things they could improve upon. This only added to their uncertainty and distress.

She knew something was wrong: "I thought I was being very thorough and conscientious, when in fact I was using the same kind of deficit model that I'd seen and heard in high school." Yet, this was the only type of pedagogy she knew as both a student and teacher.

For Jenny, this disturbing awareness was the beginning of her search for a new way to educate students. Her search would soon bring the global world closer to home. A colleague introduced Jenny to the writings of Elizabeth Jones, a well-known professor in California. Jones's work (1986, 1993, 2007) describes a constructivist approach to educating adults. As Jenny began learning about this new perspective of adult teaching, she knew she had found her answer.

Jones's work allowed Jenny to create a teaching style encouraging students to play a dynamic role in their own learning through classroom interactions and applying ideas to their own lives and experience. It valued the development of flexibility, curiosity, and creative thinking.

Jenny knew that she would need to rethink almost everything she did as an instructor. One example was her approach to each student's journal writing:

> As a result of that "wake up," I don't "mark" students' journals; instead I meet with them and discuss them, after I have heard more about their experiences.

Their stories are now in the foreground and what they write in their journals is unpacked together. I've learned to let go of "the plan" and see where students' voices could lead me.

Developing Innovative Practice

Lei's and Jenny's paths to developing innovative practice began with their first shocking experiences with the power of storytelling. It started them on the journey of moving from "depending on authority to becoming authors of their own lives" (Baxter Magolda, 2012, p. 33). Baxter Magolda describes this ability to be self-authoring, as being able to "take personal responsibility for their own beliefs and actions" (p. 33). She believes becoming self-authoring is one of the most important skills students can learn in college. But instructors must first develop it in themselves before they can pass it on to students.

For both women, this began with seeing the importance of understanding their own stories. Their next step was becoming aware of the negative effects of their traditional views and practices of teaching. Cranton (2006) believes self-awareness "provides the groundwork for transformative learning about teaching (p. 183)." A critical period for Lei and Jenny came once they decided to leave behind past beliefs and assumptions of their roles as instructors. It was in this void of undoing that they reached out for ideas beyond their past beliefs and were willing to experiment with something new. Cranton found this willingness to experiment with practice is a good way "of questioning, reflecting, and imagining alternatives" (p. 186).

Expanding Scope of Leadership

In the end, Lei and Jenny took the risk of facing the unknown and making their students' empowerment a guiding force for their work. Their break with following a traditional model of instruction opened the door to using storytelling practice in more complex ways and taking their work beyond the classroom.

Chinese Home Daycare Providers

One group of early childhood providers was palpably missing from Lei's classes. These were low-income immigrant Chinese women doing daycare in their homes. They came from various countries: China, Taiwan, Vietnam, and Hong Kong. Struggling economically, they did not speak English and were isolated from other communities. ESL classes seemed daunting.

Wanting to reach this group of providers, Lei arranged with the college to teach the women early childhood education classes in their home language. Lei was ready to make use of the translating skills she developed as an immigrant in college. Her first step in formulating this new program was to translate textbooks into the Chinese language.

Lei knew that storytelling would be important. But she understood the need to respect privacy:

> With a group of Chinese women, I did not start with storytelling. In their countries, you never tell stories to any outsiders. The first semester I had to build their trust. They were polite, but willing only to exchange information.

As the women became more comfortable with her during the first semester, Lei began sharing some personal stories about her own experience of immigrating to the USA. Listening to her struggles, they identified with her and became more open about their lives.

Eventually, the women began sharing personal experiences, initially in private with Lei. It was a sign that she was no longer an outsider. Many tragic stories emerged. One woman from Taiwan told about her stillborn child. In shock and grief, she called her husband who was living away from home for work. He didn't care, not even asking about her. Overwhelmed with despair and shame, she grabbed her two children and took them to a bridge so they could all jump off. She didn't do it, but she needed to finally tell somebody.

By the second semester, the women had developed a sense of trust as they got to know Lei and each other: "For Chinese people, everything is about relationship. And about food. The students brought wonderful traditional food to class." Lei could now fully incorporate storytelling-based teaching with them.

Organizing Chinese Home Daycare Providers

Lei watched as the barriers started dropping away. They continued taking classes and studying English as a second language. But she knew that learning English would be a long journey for these women.

Truly helping them would require going beyond her work in the classroom. She decided to start an organization designed for Chinese child care providers who have not mastered English. Lei continued using her storytelling practice. Her Chinese students keep coming to be educated. And they work together as part of their association.

The Artifact Project

Jenny knew that many colleagues would question and criticize her new approach to teaching. She decided to create a research project to show the effectiveness of this pedagogy. The "Artifact Project" (Walker, 2010) consisted of three consecutive workshops using experiential storytelling and an outside researcher to analyze and assess the results. These workshops took place over an 18-month period.

Jenny wanted to understand how experiential learning and dialogue could help to shape students' sense of self-trust, reflection, and identity as growing teachers and lifelong learners. Students were asked to bring in artifacts from their own lives, reflect upon their meaning, and connect them with relevant educational literature. Artifacts are items that have personal meaning to the students, which they can use to facilitate reflective discussion (Walker, 2010). Dialogue flowed. As the project began to unfold, Jenny watched as students took the risk of sharing their items and personal reflections with others.

Jenny's student, Molly, cautiously stood in front of the group holding her well-used copy of *The Edmonds Cookbook*. She described how important this book has been in her life. It had brought creativity and enjoyment every day. She told the group that this book represents the reality of "the rhythm of teaching...a complex journey, a journey of discovery, wonder, disappointment and fulfillment" (Ayers, 2001, p. 122). Molly explained how this was similar to her own experience as a teacher:

> As a student teacher, I feel that my own experiences and memories contribute significantly to the way I support and encourage children...I know that the care I give and my development as a teacher is a journey where I'm sure I will see situations where I will not always be able to make a difference...where some of the effort I put in may not always be enough.

Jenny was thrilled to hear how Molly's presentation sparked other students to reveal their own complicated experiences as teachers.

Mary held up her pounamu, a beautiful jade stone, to reflect on what her Maori culture means to her and how she hoped to share her values and beliefs with others in early childhood settings. She noted that this artifact represents prestige in her Maori culture, as it is handed down through generations. Mary used a quote to articulate why she chose this artifact:

> "Culturally valued ways of behaving should be respected...A multicultural community cannot afford to have silent members; we must keep learning from and about each other, to be inclusive and respectful" (Jones, 2007, p. 70). So my pounamu not only represents the Maori culture of Aotearoa, New Zealand, but also my love and passion to spread a positive outlook on the culture.

Mary's presentation, like Molly's, brought a lively discussion among the group. Many others followed, each bringing their unique insights and experiences.

Findings

Unlike Jenny's first experience with her students using a highly directive approach to teaching, the artifact project generated more expressiveness and self-reflection. The uncritical sharing and affirming of their personal histories, stories, and experiences brought a sense of empowerment and value to the students as individuals who have much to offer. These benefits extended to their ability to work with others in a more open and caring way. As one student stated, "Discovering your-self opens you to discovering others."

Fabia's Reflection   Fabia, one of Jenny's students, describes how the reflective process made her increasingly aware of her connection to others:

> It amazed me how I was able to find common threads in some value or belief among everyone. I began to understand that, although we come from differing backgrounds, we all share a common thread. We all share a common need to connect, to contribute, to be heard and acknowledged.

Fabia shares the professional benefits of her educational experiences:

> As a New Zealand European in a Samoan preschool, I was part of a minority group. I did not know about the culture, I hadn't experienced their way of life. Yet, I was so warmly welcomed and accepted from the very beginning.
>
> Through my time immersed in a new culture, I began to see the significant role entire communities and extended families play in raising and caring for a child. In these environments, the focus was not on efficient or extravagant teaching with many activities all around. Instead, all aspects of care were grounded in relationships, spending time together and sharing life together.

Fabia's reflections show more than a desire and ability to understand a very different culture. It shows how the awareness gained from being part of an educational experience that combines personal reflection and sharing with others becomes the basis for an open-minded perception of cultural differences and a willingness to contribute within their accepted values.

Conclusion

Lei's and Jenny's stories are reminders of the multitude of circumstances that can bring leadership to our field. Their paths to leadership did not come out of a supportive family. Instead, they came from years of self-protective withdrawal, searching for a glimpse of hope, and a desperate need to build a better life. It was during this process of beginning a new life that they discovered their passion for teaching and preparing early childhood educators.

Both women went through unique paths of development, both personally and professionally. They also took highly different journeys in discovering innovative approaches to early childhood teacher preparation, yet they had important traits in common. Their life experiences had brought them a deep sensitivity to the pain of being invisible and trapped within limitations of gender and societal constraints. And, each had the opportunity of becoming aware of her story from a more expanded lens, empowering each to move beyond early limitations in their lives.

As they encountered the limitations of traditional ways of teaching, Lei's and Jenny's sensitivity and awareness led them to a search for more effective ways of educating their students. Guiding them was their goal of creating a form of education that made a meaningful connection with their students. This necessitated finding ways to reach out and embrace the lives of students as part of education.

It was through understanding the personal and cultural context of their students' lives, through strategies of storytelling and active engagement in the learning process, that they were able to build a new foundation for teacher preparation. Taking this journey of letting go of the known and risking a new approach is both exciting and challenging. It is helpful to have some guidelines along the way while wondering through this unknown path.

References

Anonymous. (1984, October 13). Letters to the Editor. *Christchurch Press*.

Ayers, B. (2001). *Fugitive days: A memoir*. Boston: Beacon Press.

Baxter Magolda, M. B. (2012). Building learning partnerships. *Change*, 44(1), 32–38.

Cranton, P. (2006). *Understanding and promoting transformative learning: A guide for educators of adults*. San Francisco: Jossey-Bass.

Daloz, L., Keen, C., Keen, L., & Parks, S. (1996). *Common fire: Leading lives of commitment in a complex world*. Boston: Beacon Press.

Gonzalez, J. (2012, August 28). Young women are more likely than men to aspire to college and to graduate. *Chronicle of Higher Education*. http://chronicle.com/article/Young-Women-Are-More-Likely/133980

Jones, E. (1986). *Teaching adults: An active learning approach.* Washington, DC: National Association for the Education of Young Children.

Jones, E. (1993). Introduction. In E. Jones (Ed.), *Growing teachers: Partnerships in staff development* (pp. xii–xxii). New York: National Association for the Education of Young Children.

Jones, E. (2007). *Teaching adults revisited: Active learning for early childhood educators.* Washington, DC: National Association for the Education of Young Children.

McAdams, D. P., & McLean, K. C. (2013). Narrative identity. *Current Directions in Psychological Science, 22*(3), 233–38. doi:10.1177/0963721413475622

Paquette, D., & Ryan, D. P. (2000). Bronfenbrenner's Ecological Systems Theory. http://www.floridahealth.gov/AlternateSites/CMS-Kids/providers/early_steps/training/documents/bronfenbrenners_ecological.pdf

Preskill, S., & Brookfield, S. (2009). *Learning as a way of leading: Lessons from the struggle for social justice.* San Francisco: Jossey-Bass.

Sullivan, D. (2009). *Learning to lead: Effective leadership skills for teachers of young children* (2nd ed.). St. Paul, MN: Redleaf Press.

Walker, J. (2010). Cats, kayaks and other artefacts: Using play props to explore reflective practice. *The Space, 22* (Summer), 12–13.

Chapter 7

My Journey as an Instructor

The very nature of early childhood education demands continuous growth and learning. In the dynamically unfolding world of human development, there are no pat answers we can hold onto without risking our ability to reach others. What worked effectively yesterday with a child or adult may no longer work today. An educational theory we used for many years may become an obstacle with a group whose beliefs are counter to what we studied in all our textbooks.

Given the uncertain nature of our work, how can we continue to learn and grow and help others to do the same? Are there principles and guidelines we can follow? Teachers, directors, trainers, and college instructors all face the challenge of being part of a field rife with constant uncertainty. Through my own story as an instructor, in this chapter I explore fundamental principles that can be used for ongoing professional growth as well as for teaching others.

The classroom scenarios and life stories presented in previous chapters show the powerful and transformative effects of a storytelling-based practice. Students' stories and interactions have brought the real world into our classroom, and with it a rich and complex curriculum. I have felt a deep sense of excitement witnessing students engaged in the hard work of becoming self-aware, thoughtful, and expressive people who have an understanding of multiple realities beyond their own lives.

These are abilities they will need in order to work effectively with the many kinds of unexpected conditions facing children and families today. Britzman (2000) believes that "teacher education has not yet grappled with a theory of knowledge that can analyze social fractures, profound social violence, decisions of disregard, and how from such devastations, psychological significance can be made" (p. 200). Storytelling practice was designed to prepare students with the kind of knowledge, skills, and awareness needed to grapple with such conditions. Yet, even as I embraced storytelling as my teaching model, this new practice continued to bring challenges for me as an instructor.

Understanding Myself

Implementing a storytelling practice presented an entirely new perspective on education. Students' lives and experiences would now play a major role in our unfolding curriculum. This challenged my most basic assumptions of learning, the role of students, the role of instructors, and the culture of institutions of higher education. Similar to students going through their own process of transformative development, I also needed to create a new frame of mind that would enable me to make use of this practice.

Reconfiguring my role as an instructor has necessitated asking myself critical questions: What hidden assumptions impede my ability to work with students within a less structured, more expansive curriculum? What new skills and awareness will I need to develop? How can I support myself as I venture into unknown territory, and take risks in trying new ideas? Just as we ask our students to become reflective practitioners, we need to do the same.

Becoming a Reflective Instructor

Having successfully gone through the school system, I still hold many beliefs about education: gaining more information makes us smarter; do not let anything interfere with the classroom agenda; the instructor and textbook have all the answers that students will need to learn and succeed.

My crooked path to self-awareness was a reminder that learning is not a linear or simple journey. It is filled with progress and retreat—new awareness, then regression, growth, then resistance—all the while moving ahead. I needed a variety of tools to support my development as a reflective instructor. Below are some tools that I have used for ongoing self-reflection and growth.

Teaching Journal

The greatest source of my learning has taken place through journal writing. I find that by focusing on real events that occurred in the classroom that day, particularly those that have intense emotional overtones, I can learn more about my assumptions of teaching than by making an abstract list.

After a class session in understanding children and parents, I did some reflective writing on a discussion that did not have positive results for me or members of the class. It left me feeling upset and confused about my part in this negative outcome. We were engaged in a lively discussion about an observation assignment the students had just completed. It quickly moved from individual reports to an engaging dialogue. After one student reported questioning the way teachers hover over children always ready to intervene, another student expressed disagreement. She came to a different conclusion from her observations. She believes that teachers were making use of "teachable moments" to give the children needed skills. More students joined the discussion, making it highly complex, intense, and informative.

As the dialogue progressed, I vaguely noticed my attention moving from engagement to the timing of my agenda for the evening. I began ignoring the excitement and importance of issues being discussed.

I had further plans for the evening. I began cutting people off and abruptly ending conversations. I watched a student's face lose all animation when I interrupted her, saying, "We don't have any more time for this. We need to move on." Picking up on my impatience, the tone of the discussion lost its vitality. Everybody was shutting down.

Outside the pressure of the moment, I could see how my attitude had shifted and its dramatic effect on the students. Usually I am able to flow with the delicate balance between my agenda and vital issues that need to be discussed. Once again, I could see how difficult it was for me to move from a carefully planned agenda to the messy dynamics of interactive learning.

I was particularly dismayed because we had been discussing the importance of facilitating an emergent curriculum with children. I realized I had been modeling the biggest roadblock to having this happen, allowing my prescheduled agenda to take over.

Student Feedback

Following my journal writing, I read over students' "End of the Evening" writing. Feedback from students has been particularly helpful in revealing ways that I still bring unconscious beliefs into the classroom. For every class, I have a handout for feedback. It uses a variety of categories for responses, depending upon the course. Some common questions I ask: "What did you find most interesting? Did anything confuse, frustrate or bore you? What new connections did you make during class? Is there anything you want me to know?" I respond to their remarks with acknowledgment and supportive comments to encourage the students to continue giving honest feedback.

Student feedback clearly reflected the way my actions had affected them during our class discussion. Their statements ranged from being mildly upset, "I was disappointed we could not continue the discussion," to anger, "I felt like you were cutting students down at the knees." From the honesty of their remarks, I was able to see the results of unexamined assumptions I still held about teaching. It also gave me a chance to individually respond to students' concerns.

Collaborative Faculty Learning

When I told a faculty colleague about this class experience, I received the coaching I needed to make use of it as part of our curriculum. She suggested that I can be a role model for my students by sharing with them my own process of learning. From our discussion, I realized this would be an opportunity to share with the students how easily and unsuspectingly old patterns can show up.

I was also aware of how easy it is for me as a college instructor to prepare my work in isolation, never considering the value of sharing ideas, concerns, or problems with trusted colleagues. Just as students gain new perspectives from dialogue with each other, this same process can occur among instructors or other professional colleagues.

Collaborative Learning Within the Classroom

At our next class, I revealed my discomfort after our last class, and the importance of self-reflection. I told my students that something did not feel right about my responses to them during our discussion of observations. Reading their "End of the Evening" writings allowed me to see more clearly what had taken place that evening and its effects on our learning process.

I talked with the class about the "bubble" concept of how deep-seated beliefs can form a bubble around our thinking and forcefully emerge with little conscious awareness (Pollner, 1987). I was now aware that this is what happened to me during our last class. As we continued discussing this idea, I noticed students nodding their heads in agreement. They began sharing their own experience of having unconscious beliefs come up for them. Everyone wanted to know how to deal with this.

Since we were working with deep-seated beliefs, I decided to do an experiential activity around this concept. I asked everyone to close their eyes and think about a time they judged somebody and later realized they had been wrong. I asked them to think back to what beliefs they held about this person. And what happened that changed their view?

After the inner reflection, students began to share about ways they had unconsciously reacted to children, parents, and colleagues. Chris said that she thought about a parent she was assigned to work with as a parenting counselor for Head Start. She did not like the parent at all. She felt this woman was too opinionated, loud, and not acting the way Chris is comfortable with in relationships. Chris became very cold and matter-of-fact in working with this parent. But, as she got to know her better, she realized that she was delightful and that her forcefulness came out of feeling distrust and uncertainty with a person in authority like herself. Chris added that she had become aware of this woman's defenses from her own reflections on ways she dealt with situations that felt threatening to her. Now she realizes how quickly her beliefs can come up.

Listening to their experiences, I decided to do further work with this issue. I had the class break into small groups and brainstorm ways they can catch themselves when "bubbles of beliefs" come up. Twenty minutes later, we reconvened and each group shared their ideas with the class. One group reported that it is helpful to pay attention when negative reactions occur, then to journal about it and see what beliefs had come up. Another group said that talking with a trusted co-worker after a difficult experience can help a teacher better understand what happened.

The thoughtful sharing in each group affirmed for me the value of collaborative work with students from my own experience. This kind of collaboration is an important skill for early childhood educators. West-Olatunji, Behar-Horenstein, and Rant (2008) in their research with preschool teachers found the value of meeting weekly to share lesson studies they developed for children. When problems with implementation were revealed, the group process led to the emergence of creativity and new ideas, along with an increase in collegiality and mutual support among the teachers.

Shifting Pedagogy

As a new college instructor, I did not receive formal training in how to teach. Like most instructors, I incorporated the values, techniques, and strategies used by institutions of higher education. This was largely an authoritarian model of education, in which I was the expert whose job it was to fill the minds of students with knowledge. Students played a passive role of absorbing and proving to me they learned the course material (Adamson & Bailie, 2012). Implementing a storytelling practice has entailed radically changing my vision of education. This has meant letting go of previous structures that provided me with a sense of certainty as an instructor.

An Action Plan for an Evening's Class

When I use student stories as a focus, classroom learning becomes a landscape of ever- changing dynamics, unexpected content, and intense emotional expression that are all part of human life. Within such uncertainty, Shulman (2005) recommends having a routine by using a learning protocol. It provides a secure structure within which uncertain and unpredictable content can be welcomed with reduced anxiety. Following this advice, I offer students in my classes a transparent routine, handing out an agenda at each of our meetings. Here is an example of an agenda and a reflective format expanded from my initial work with nontraditional students (Bernheimer, 2003):

Class/Date
Participatory activity to begin class session

- Examples: Discussion/questions of current assignments or student presentation with feedback.

Short lecture: Current topic/reading assignment
Class discussion: Possible prompts

- What was most valuable for you in assigned reading?
- Was there a story from the reading that you could relate to in your life?
- Was there anything you disagree with from the reading?

Personal reflection on key concept (e.g., stereotyping, self-esteem, etc.):

- What happened? How did it make you feel?
- Were there decisions you made about yourself or others from this experience?
- Followed by paired sharing

Small groups: Have somebody take notes. Discuss the following.

• Share your personal experience of concept. How did this affect you? Share one example with class.
• What did you learn from this experience? Share one example with class.
• Share and select one child you know who has been affected by this concept. Describe this child, including what happened. How is this child reacting? What could you do as a teacher to help this child?

Class sharing
End of the Evening writing
Description of items on agenda

Participatory activity to begin class session: I often begin class with some type of activity or discussion, which actively engages students. This could range from reviewing current or upcoming assignments in which students can clarify or ask questions. Or begin class with a student presentation and feedback.

Short lecture: I use a short lecture (approximately15 minutes), which I hone down from more extensive ones I previously used as an instructor. My purpose is to bring out important insights and underlying dynamics rather than repeating information that is part of their reading.

Class discussion: After a brief introduction to the topic, a variety of ways can be used to discuss the ideas and apply them to students' life experiences. These may include open dialogue, personal reflection, and group activities. Once the classroom is infused with real-life events, my role as an instructor must concurrently shift to one of participant and facilitator.

Personal reflection on key concept: Personal reflections enable students to fully understand how a concept applies to their lives. These are private reflections. They are not asked to turn them in. This is followed by either paired or group sharing. Students have been told that sharing their reflection is a choice, not a requirement.

Small groups: Small-group activities are designed to take learning to a more complex level. Provocative questions bring out a variety of experiences and lead to in-depth discussions. The group activity ends with ways to apply the idea to their work with children and families.

End of the Evening writing: The End of the Evening writing provides immediate feedback on how a student has experienced the class session. It also allows students to share something they feel I should be aware of in their lives. This enables me to have personal communication with each student as well as making possible revisions to my curriculum.

Guidelines for Interaction

Using a storytelling practice includes the sharing of personal information, expressing opinions, and engaging in open-ended dialogue. This level of interaction requires a sense of safety and respectful communication among the participants. For many students, this may be the first time in their lives that their opinions are included as part of the learning process. Discussing the concepts of confidentiality and respectful listening sets the stage for a safe, productive learning environment.

Confidentiality

When beginning a new course, I share information about the challenging nature of work as an early childhood educator and the importance of confidentiality as part of our classroom interactions—whatever is shared in class is done for the purpose of learning and should remain within the classroom. I find students are relieved at hearing this and dedicated to upholding the safety of the class environment.

Respectful Listening

A second tenet of the class is respectful listening. I describe this as attentively listening to and understanding what is being shared, whether or not they agree with it. I discuss the importance of this ability as an essential tool for effective communication within the classroom as well as in their professional work.

Principles for Implementing a Storytelling Practice

One aspect of my shifting role as an instructor was learning the skills needed to support a highly participatory, living classroom. In the following, I outline principles that I found supportive in facilitating a dynamic learning environment.

Principle #1: Creating a Learning Community

When beginning a new class, my primary goal is to provide a welcoming atmosphere and supportive context for a storytelling practice.

Getting to Know Each Other

An introductory exercise allows students to get to know each other, thereby establishing the necessary conditions for interactive storytelling. I use an introductory exercise when starting a new class.

The first part of the exercise has students share a little about themselves. The second part asks students to answer a question that relates to the particular subject matter for the class. For example, for a class focusing on children's development within the context of their family, I ask students to share one thing they liked and one thing they did not like about growing up within their family.

I begin by sharing relevant facts about myself, including some personal struggles. I tell them about my family of origin, sharing how much I enjoyed being raised as part of a large extended family. However, this was also difficult for me as a quiet and introverted child who enjoyed spending time alone. My sharing is purposeful. It is my first move away from a separated role as the professional expert into one of shared dialogue. Depending upon the number of students, I have found this exercise takes anywhere from 20 to 30 minutes.

Examples of Introductory Exercises

Depending upon the curriculum of the class, these are a few opening introductions that I have used:

- Share with us a story about your name. What does it mean to you? How do you feel about it?
- Tell us a valuable strength and weakness that came out of the family you were raised in.
- Share about a time in your life when you realized the importance of health, safety, and nutrition.

A Context for Learning

Most students enter this field with the desire to make a contribution to our society. I reinforce this commitment by reminding them that they have the opportunity to provide a nurturing foundation for every child's life. I then discuss how this particular course is designed to provide knowledge and skills they will need in their work.

Principle #2: Being Mindful of Classroom Environment

Since discussions are often filled with emotionally charged issues, it is important for the instructor to develop an awareness of group dynamics and skills for using these to deepen the learning experience.

Allow Time for Open Dialogue

A topic that brings up emotional tension in the room holds much value for the learning process. During these discussions, I pay close attention to indicators of intense emotional involvement. These include facial expressions, eye contact, and tone of voice that reveal strong feelings and students' need for further discussion.

Principle #3: Support Each Story to Be a Vision for Growth

Empathetic Listening

Empathy is the ability to understand the other person on both an intellectual and emotional level. As students share and listen to multiple stories in the classroom, including their triumphs and failures, they deepen their empathetic understanding of others. My role as the instructor is to model empathetic listening.

Stories and Learning

For continuous growth, students need to learn to see difficult experiences as part of their learning process. Mayes (2005) discusses the critical role of the instructor in reframing failure as a prelude to success. During classroom dialogue, I consciously support students to reshape their perception of negative events in order to see them as a necessary part of their growth. This ability to learn from experience is an important disposition for early childhood educators who need to be like researchers constantly testing hypotheses (Jones, 2007).

Conclusion

Although this journey is about my development as a college instructor as I shifted my approach to teaching adults, all of us in early childhood education face similar challenges. I needed to become a more reflective, interactive instructor. Program directors and teachers of children need to build similar skills as they grow and adapt to new conditions facing them every day. Reflective journal writing, collaborating with trusted colleagues on difficult issues, and receiving feedback from families can enhance our ability to effectively work with new circumstances.

The value of storytelling functions well beyond the confines of a classroom. Purposeful sharing of stories in a safe environment can bring about both deeper understanding among staff and the development of a supportive community. The recommended classroom guidelines of confidentiality and respectful listening are also valuable for early childhood programs, enhancing the quality of all interactions from communicating with parents to staff meetings and professional development.

Over the years, the principles described in this chapter have enabled me to make use of my teaching experiences to continue moving towards greater mastery in using a storytelling practice. I have also come to see the greater implications of this practice as our world takes its own faltering steps into a deeply intertwined and uncertain future.

References

Adamson, C., & Bailie, J. (2012). Education vs. learning: Restorative practices in higher education. *Journal of Transformative Education*, 10 (3) 139–56.

Bernheimer, S. (2003). *New possibilities for early childhood education: Stories from our non-traditional students.* New York: Peter Lang.

Britzman, D. (2000). Teacher education in the confusion of our times. *Journal of Teacher Education*, 5(3), 163–202.

Jones, E. (2007). *Teaching adults revisited: Active learning for early childhood educators.* Washington, DC: National Association for the Education of Young Children.

Mayes, C. (2005). *Education and Jung: Elements of an archetypal pedagogy.* Lanham, MD: Rowman & Littlefield Education.

Pollner, M. (1987). *Mundane reason: Reality in everyday and sociological discourse.* Cambridge: Cambridge University Press.

Shulman, L. (2005). Pedagogies of uncertainty. *Liberal Education*, *91*(2). http://www.aacu.org/publications-research/periodicals/pedagogies-uncertainty

West-Olatunji, C., Behar-Horenstein, L., & Rant, J. (2008). Mediated lesson study, collaborative learning, and cultural competence among early childhood educators. *Journal of Research in Childhood Education*, *23*(1), 96–98.

Chapter 8

A Changing World

Walking into the classroom, I look around at the faces of my students, whom I have come to know so well. They are talking and laughing together. Some smile and wave to me as I enter the class. Delicious-looking food items line the back table for our final pot-luck celebration. This is our last class of the semester.

Scanning the room, I think of their many stories, struggles, and hard-earned wisdom. I'm looking forward to hearing their final thoughts on the class. Their sharing will lead the way for our curriculum tonight. As we begin, Sophia raises her hand to speak. With tears in her eyes, she quietly looks at each student. Hers will be the first of many unexpected reflections:

> You know, all the readings and projects were great. But what I really learned from this class is that I've been living in a box. I couldn't see beyond my real-ity. My own biases blocked me from knowing anybody different from myself, even people in my own family. I just want to thank each of you for telling your stories. Every story shocked me. I thought I had everyone figured out when I first looked at you. But I didn't know anything that you all had been through, how brave you are, and how much you cared about me when I finally could

tell the truth about my own life. I feel like I'm going back into the world knowing less than when I came into this class. The one thing I know is that everybody has a story, and I can't judge anyone without knowing their story.

Ron talks about how his previous identity began falling apart in this class:

Growing up, I was taught to be an all-American boy. I thought I knew who I was as a guy. I had to be strong, handle any problems, and fight it out with anybody who came up against me. And for sure, I couldn't be caught crying or having emotions. But, hearing your stories, something changed in me. I remember Tommy holding up a picture of himself as an emaciated little boy, living in a refugee camp. Tears started coming; I couldn't stop them. I was so embarrassed. I looked around, afraid people would laugh at me. But nobody did and it was okay.

Even as a teacher, I thought I knew what was best for the children. I was the expert. That began falling apart the day I shared about my battle with the director, when she told me a father didn't want me to change his infant daughter. I could only see my side. I was right, and he was wrong. Hearing your responses, I started to question myself for the first time. I never thought I'd be glad to not have all the answers. Today, I'm leaving here with a new kind of uncertainty. And I'm glad.

As I listen to their sharing, I notice they all include a sense of disequilibrium. I realize this class has been as much about undoing old beliefs as learning new information. It is clear the students have been engaged in the difficult process of formulating a new context for their lives and their work as early childhood educators. They are shifting their perspectives from making sure people fit their picture of the correct way to pushing against their own limitations and beliefs that disconnect them from others. They are clearing the way for a new, more complex vision.

Their perceptions are a reminder of the importance of constructing and reconstructing one's self to meet the needs of new situations we encounter. Bruner (2004) points out how our self-making stories accumulate over time. But these get out of date, because our self-making stories need to be revised to fit the changing circumstances in the world. The shifting perceptions of students in this class may be their greatest asset as early childhood educators today.

A recent article in the *Los Angeles Times* by Boyle (2015) provides a glimpse into the changing and often desperate realities of people's lives at this time. An incident took place far from Los Angeles. Yet, it is similar to the quality of distress many early childhood educators encounter in their work anywhere.

The incident began at a French port where people were lined up in cars to board the ferries taking them across the English Channel. Traffic was severely jammed because ferry workers were going on strike for fear of job losses. Large groups of migrants, primarily from North Africa and the Middle East, started trying to break into cars and trucks trapped in long lines at the ferry terminal in an attempt to get to England. The article clearly describes the distress felt by all parties: ferry workers fearful of losing their jobs; migrants desperate to get to a place where they could work and live in safety; frightened passengers caught in a global drama that suddenly touched their lives.

Early Childhood at the Crux of Change

As the postindustrial era continues to move ahead and traditional ways of living are being left behind, a web of change is weaving itself across our world. Uncertainty is quickly replacing the known. The disruptive effects are being felt in countries, communities, family life, religion, and employment.

The nature of these disruptions is perplexing and filled with contradictory dynamics. The saga in France reveals more than a conflict of differing needs. It symbolizes a frightening social, political, and economic breakdown, in which all parties are at risk. While the Internet and worldwide economic ties have created global connections at an unprecedented level, increasing numbers of people feel invisible and powerless. The repercussions are frightening: terrorism, revolutions, economic collapse, desperate migrants.

Amidst the unpredictable changes taking place, education has risen as a focal point of hope. Whether they are living in distant villages, major cities, or suburban neighborhoods, parents know that education will be a key to their children's success in our world. In particular, early childhood is recognized as foundational for a child's educational journey. This new reality is behind a worldwide expansion of early childhood programs. Governments, employers, local communities, and researchers over the past 30 years have been paying increasing attention to programs serving young children (Dahlberg, Moss, & Pence, 2007).

Danger and Promise

The dangers facing early childhood education lie in the very outcomes that often go along with professional recognition. Together with early childhood education's increasing importance, and financial investment in this field by government and businesses, comes a demand for accountability—for universal, measurable criteria to evaluate programs. Unfortunately, these criteria are still based on traditional Western concepts of child development and school performance. These do not match the highly complex and chaotic changes taking place throughout our culture, as I describe at length in this book. These are changes that demand new types of skills and relationships (Dahlberg et al., 2007).

Within the unresolved issues currently facing early childhood education lies the possibility of a future vision that fits this time of rapid change. It is through our programs that vulnerable young children and their parents are introduced to the world of education. For the families we serve, our field sits at the cutting edge of a delicate balance between fear and exclusion, on the one hand, and the beginning of a hopeful future, on the other hand. Our programs will either reinforce labels and categories of those who will succeed and those left behind or create an expansive new view of learning, community and civil society.

A New Legacy for Early Childhood Education

Leaving the classroom on our last night, I remember the stories of childhood the students bravely shared throughout the semester. Few of their stories fit my ideal picture of healthy development. Whether it was hearing about the quiet pain of a child inside a perfect-looking family, the feelings of being lost and uprooted from immigration, or the suffering from abuse by schoolmates for looking different, each student's story added to a deeper understanding of development. Their stories went far beyond textbook theories.

Within the hidden pain in students' lives, there were always many unexpected forms of resilience, illuminating the strength of the human spirit. The recognition of this resilience often emerged as other students attentively listened and responded about the ways each story taught them important insights, generating admiration of the person's strength. It was clear that students were learning what it means to respect and care for others beyond appearances and differences.

I realize that storytelling practice does more than bring the real world into our classroom. Students are being educated for a greater purpose than simply enacting a curriculum. They are learning that education is about healing our world. Their stories present a fuller picture of development—one that does not back away from addressing the problems and tragedies in our world. In this time of tremendous social breakdown, Britzman (2000) believes that only through understanding what has gone wrong can education regain its relevancy.

Vision for a Changing World

For early childhood educators this new world raises new questions. Will our programs combat the dehumanization of marginalized citizens in our world? How can we prepare teachers to understand and empathize with today's students, both mainstream and those who are different?

This book attends to these issues through the use of the students' stories. A storytelling paradigm broadens the scope of learning, addressing critical issues of complex relations, connections with others, and the development of empathy. The classroom format models the qualities they will need to bring into their work as early childhood educators: open sharing, honest reflection, and creative solutions. These are the skills that will prepare them to change with the changing times.

Thus, our field can take its rightful role in the world as a source of both knowledge and healing.

A very brave 17-year-old girl and Nobel Peace Laureate, Malala Yousafzai, in Pakistan, expresses the full implications of the potential education holds in our world today:

> If you want to end the war then, instead of sending guns, send books. Instead of sending tanks, send pens. Instead of sending soldiers, send teachers. (Yousafzai, n.d.)

References

Boyle, C. (2015, June 24). Strike, migrants disrupt channel crossing. *Los Angeles Times*, p. A6.

Britzman, D. (2000). Teacher education in the confusion of our times. *Journal of Teacher Education, 5* (3), 163–202.

Bruner, Jerome (2004). The narrative creation of self. In E. Lynne & A. McLeod (Eds.), *The handbook of narrative psychotherapy: Practice, theory, and research* (pp. 3–14). Thousand Oaks, CA: Sage.

Dahlberg, G., Moss, P., & Pence, A. (2007). *Beyond quality in early childhood education and care: Language of evaluation.* New York: Routledge.

Yousafzai, M. (n.d.). The Peace Alliance. http://peacealliance.org/tools-education/peace-inspirational-quotes/#sthash.e43klQGw.dpuf

References

Adamson, C. & Bailie, J. (2012). Education vs. learning: Restorative practices in higher education. *Journal of Transformative Education, 10* (3) 139–56.

Anonymous. (1984, October 13). Letters to the Editor. *Christchurch Press.*

Argyris, C. (1974). Alternative schools: A behavioral analysis. *Harvard Educational Review, 41*(4), 550–67.

Ayers, B. (2001). *Fugitive days: A memoir.* Boston: Beacon Press.

Bateson, M. (1995). *Peripheral visions: Learning along the way.* New York: Harper Perennial Publishing.

Baxter Magolda, M. B. (2012). Building learning partnerships. *Change, 44*(1), 32–38.

Beatty, B. (1995). *Preschool education in America: The culture of young children from the Colonial era to the present.* New Haven, CT: Yale University Press.

Bell, S. (2012, March 8). Nontraditional students are the new majority. http://lj.libraryjournal.com/2012/03/opinion/steven-bell/nontraditional-students-are-the-new-majority-from-the-bell-tower

Bernheimer, S. (2003). *New possibilities for early childhood education: Stories from our nontraditional students.* New York: Peter Lang.

Bernheimer, S. (2005). Telling our stories: A key to effective teaching. *Exchange Magazine, 162*(March/April), 82–83.

Bernheimer, S., & Jones, E. (2013). The gifts of the stranger. *Young Children, 68*(4), 62–67.

Boyle, C. (2015, June 24). Strike, migrants disrupt channel crossing. *Los Angeles Times,* p. A6.

Britzman, D. (2000). Teacher education in the confusion of our times. *Journal of Teacher Education*, 5(3), 163–202.

Brookfield, S. (1995). *Becoming a critically reflective teacher.* San Francisco: Jossey-Bass.

Brown, M. W. (2006). *The runaway bunny.* New York: HarperCollins.

Brownlee, J., & Berthelsen, D. (2006). Personal epistemology and relational pedagogy in early childhood teacher education programs. *Early Years: An International Journal of Research*, 2(1), 17–29.

Bruner, Jerome (2004). The narrative creation of self. In E. Lynne & A. McLeod (Eds.), *The handbook of narrative psychotherapy: Practice, theory, and research* (pp. 3–14). Thousand Oaks: Sage.

Carter, M., & Curtis, D. (2002). *Training teachers: A harvest of theory and practice.* St. Paul, MN: Redleaf Press.

Carter, M., & Curtis, D. (2009). *The visionary director: A handbook for dreaming, organizing and improving your center* (2nd ed.). St. Paul, MN: Redleaf Press.

Cavarero, A. (2005). *For more than one voice: Toward a philosophy of vocal expression.* Redwood City, CA: Stanford University Press.

Choy, S. (2002). Nontraditional undergraduates: U.S. Department of Education, National Center for Educational Statistics. http://nces.ed.gov/pubs2002/2002012.pdf

Clark, M. C., & Rossiter, M. (2008). Narrative learning in adult life. *New Directions for Adult and Continuing Education*, (119), 61–70.

Cochron, M. (2011). International perspectives on early childhood education. *Educational Policy*, 25, 65–91.

Cohen, P. (2014). Family diversity is the new normal for American children. *Council on Contemporary Families.* Retrieved September 15, 2014, from https://contemporary families.org/the-new-normal

Couldry, N. (2004). In the place of a common culture, what? *The Review of Education Pedagogy & Cultural Studies*, 1(January–March), 3–22.

Cranton, P. (2006). *Understanding and promoting transformative learning: A guide for educators of adults.* San Francisco: Jossey-Bass.

Dahlberg, G., Moss, P., & Pence, A. (2007). *Beyond quality in early childhood education and care: Language of evaluation.* New York: Routledge.

Dale, M. (2004). Tales in and out of school. In D. Liston & J. Garrison (Eds.), *Teaching, learning, and loving: Reclaiming passion in educational practice* (pp. 65–84). New York: RoutledgeFalmer.

Daloz, L., Keen, C., Keen, L., & Parks, S. (1996). *Common fire: Leading lives of commitment in a complex world.* Boston: Beacon Press.

Day, J., & Tappan, M. (1996). The narrative approach to moral development: From the epistemic subject to dialogical selves. *Human Development*, 29(2), 67–82.

Delpit, L. (2006). *Other people's children: Cultural conflict in the classroom.* New York: The New Press.

Derman-Sparks, L., & The ABC Task Force (1989). *Anti-bias curriculum: Tools for empowering young children.* Washington, DC: National Association for the Education of Young Children.

Derman-Sparks, L., & Olsen, E. J. (2012*). Anti-bias for young children and ourselves.* Washington, DC: National Association for the Education of Young Children.

Dominice, P. (2000). *Learning from our lives: Using biographies with adults.* San Francisco: Jossey-Bass.

Elliot, E. (2007). *We're not robots: The voices of daycare providers.* New York: SUNY Press.

Exposito, S., & Bernheimer, S. (2012). Non-traditional students and institutions of higher education: A conceptual framework. *Journal of Early Childhood Teacher Education, 33*, 178–89.

Freire, P. (1998). Pedagogy of the oppressed: The fear of freedom. In A. Freire & D. Macedo (Eds.), *The Paulo Freire reader* (pp. 45–66). New York: Continuum.

Ginsburg, H., & Opper, S. (1988). *Piaget's theory of intellectual development.* Englewood Cliffs, NJ: Prentice Hall.

Goleman, D. (1994). *Emotional intelligence.* New York: Bantam Books.

Gonzalez, J. (2012, August 28). Young women are more likely than men to aspire to college and to graduate. *Chronicle of Higher Education.* http://chronicle.com/article/Young-Women-Are-More-Likely/133980

Gonzalez-Mena, J. (2007). *Diversity in early care and education: Honoring differences* (5th ed.). Dubuque, IA: McGraw-Hill Education.

Heath, S. B. (1983). *Ways with words: Language, life and work in communities and classrooms.* Cambridge: Cambridge University Press.

Hillman, J. (1967). *In search: Psychology and religion.* Woodstock, CT: Spring Publications.

Jones, E. (1986). *Teaching adults: An active learning approach.* Washington, DC: National Association for the Education of Young Children.

Jones, E. (1993). Introduction. In E. Jones (Ed.), *Growing teachers: Partnerships in staff development* (pp. xii–xxii). New York: National Association for the Education of Young Children.

Jones, E. (2007). *Teaching adults revisited: Active learning for early childhood educators.* Washington, DC: National Association for the Education of Young Children.

Katz, L. (2008). *Challenges and dilemmas of educating teachers of young children.* http://www.naecte.org/docs/Katz%20Opening%20Address.pdf

Kessler, R. (2004). Grief as a gateway to love in teaching. In D. Liston & J. Garrison (Eds.). *Teaching, learning, and loving: Reclaiming passion in educational practice* (pp. 137–52). New York: RoutledgeFalmer.

Matsen, A. (2014). Global perspectives on resilience in children and youth. *Child Development, 85*(1), 6–20.

Mayes, C. (2005). *Education and Jung: Elements of an archetypal pedagogy.* Lanham, MD: Rowman & Littlefield Education.

McAdams, D. P., & McLean, K. C. (2013). Narrative identity. *Current Directions in Psychological Science, 22* (3), 233–38. doi:10.1177/0963721413475622

McDevitt, M., & Ormrod, J. (2008). Fostering conceptual change about child development in prospective teachers and other college students. *Child Development Perspectives*, 2 (2), 85–91.

McDrury, J., & Alterio, M. (2002). *Learning through storytelling in higher education: Using reflection and experience to improve learning.* Wellington, New Zealand: The Dunmore Press.

Mezirow, J. (2003). Transformative learning as discourse. *Journal of Transformative Education*, 1(1), 58–63.

Moon, J., & Flower, J. (2008). There is a story to be told…A framework for the conception of story in higher education and professional development. *Nurse Education Today*, 28(2), 232–39.

Nesteruk, O., & Marks, L. D. (2011). Parenting in immigration: Experiences of mothers and fathers from Eastern Europe raising children in the United States. *Journal of Comparative Family Studies*, 42(6), 809–25.

Palmer, P. (2007). *The courage to teach: Exploring the inner landscape of a teacher's life* (10th ed.). San Francisco: Jossey-Bass.

Paquette, D., & Ryan, D. P. (2000). Bronfenbrenner's Ecological Systems Theory. http://www.floridahealth.gov/AlternateSites/CMS-Kids/providers/early_steps/training/documents/bronfenbrenners_ecological.pdf

Perks, R., & Thomson, A. (2006). *The oral history reader* (2nd ed.). New York: Routledge.

Pew Research Center (2013). Intermarriage on the rise in the U.S. http://pewresearch.org/…/intermarriage-on-the-rise

Pittard, M. (2003). Developing identity: The transition from student to teacher. Paper presented at the Annual Meeting of the American Educational Research Association. http://files.eric.ed.gov/fulltext/ED481729.pdf

Pollner, M. (1987). *Mundane reason: Reality in everyday and sociological discourse.* Cambridge: Cambridge University Press.

Preskill, S., & Brookfield, S. (2009). *Learning as a way of leading: Lessons from the struggle for social justice.* San Francisco: Jossey-Bass.

Ricoeur, P., & Blarney, K. (1995). *Oneself as another.* Chicago: University of Chicago Press.

Saunders, D. (2010). *Arrival city: How the largest migration in history is reshaping our world.* New York: Random House.

Shuck, B., Albornoz, C., & Winberg M. (2013). Emotions and their effect on adult learning: A constructivist perspective. http://digitalcommons.fiu.edu/cgi/viewcontent.cgi?article=1270&context=sferc

Shulman, L. (2005). Pedagogies of uncertainty. *Liberal Education*, 91(2). http://www.aacu.org/publications-research/periodicals/pedagogies-uncertainty

Stott, F. (1995). Transformational leadership. In E. Jones (Ed.), *Topics in early childhood* (pp. 18–24). St. Paul, MN: Redleaf Press.

Suarez-Orozco, C., & Suarez-Orozco, M. M. (2002). *Children of immigration.* Cambridge, MA: Harvard University Press.

Suarez-Orozco, C., & Suarez-Orozco, M. M. (2010). *Learning in a new land: Immigrant students in American society.* Cambridge, MA: Belknap Press.

Sullivan, D. (2009). *Learning to lead: Effective leadership skills for teachers of young children* (2nd ed.). St. Paul, MN: Redleaf Press.

Tobin, J., Hsueh, Y., & Karasawa, M. (2009). *Preschool in three cultures revisited: China, Japan, and the United States.* Chicago: University of Chicago Press.

U.S. Census Bureau (2012). Census Bureau reports national mover rate increases after a record low in 2011. Retrieved December 10, 2012, from https://www.census.gov/newsroom/releases/archives/mobility_of_the_population/cb12-240.html

Vygotsky, L. S. (1997). *Educational psychology.* Boca Raton, FL: St. Lucie Press.

Walker, J. (2010). Cats, kayaks and other artefacts: Using play props to explore reflective practice. *The Space, 22* (Summer), 12–13.

Weber, E. (1984). *Ideas influencing early childhood education: A theoretical analysis.* New York: Teachers College Press.

West-Olatunji, C., Behar-Horenstein, L., & Rant, J. (2008). Mediated lesson study, collaborative learning, and cultural competence among early childhood educators. *Journal of Research in Childhood Education, 23* (1), 96–98.

Witherell, C. (1991). The self in narrative: A journey into paradox. In C. Witherell & N. Noddings (Eds.), *Stories lives tell: Narrative and dialogue in education* (pp. 83–95). New York: Teachers College Press.

Wood, Diane (2000). Narrating professional development: Teachers' stories as texts for improving practice. *Anthropology and Education Quarterly,* 31(4), 426–48.

World Population Review (2015). Los Angeles population. Retrieved September 10, 2015, from http://worldpopulationreview.com/us-cities/los-angeles-population

Yousafzai, M. (n.d.).The Peace Alliance. http://peacealliance.org/tools-education/peace-inspirational-quotes/#sthash.e43klQGw.dpuf

Index

CHILDHOOD STUDIES

Gaile S. Cannella, *General Editor*

For many years, the field of Childhood Studies has crossed disciplinary boundaries that include, but are not limited to, anthropology, art, education, history, humanities, and sociology by addressing diverse histories, cultures, forms of representation, and conceptualizations of "childhood". The publications in the Rethinking Childhood series have supported this work by challenging the universalization of childhood and introducing reconceptualized, critical spaces from which increased social justice and possibilities are generated for those who are younger.

This newly named Childhood Studies series in the global twenty-first century is created to continue this focus on social justice for those who are younger, but also to broaden and further explore conceptualizations of privilege, justice, possibility, responsibility, and activism. Authors are encouraged to consider "childhood" from within a context that would decenter human privilege and acknowledge environmental justice and the more-than-human Other, while continuing to research, act upon, and transform beliefs, public policy, societal institutions, and possibilities for ways of living/being in the world for all of us. Boundary crossings are of greater importance than ever as we live unprecedented technological change, violence against living beings that are not labeled human (through experimentation, industrialization, and medicine), plundering of the earth, and gaps between the privileged and the marginalized (whether rich/poor, human/nonhuman). Along with continued concerns related to social justice, equity, poverty, and diversity, some authors in the Childhood Studies series will choose to think about, and ask questions such as: What does it mean to be a younger human being within such a world? What are the values, education, and forms of care provided within this context? Can/how should these dispositions and practices be transformed? Can childhood studies, and the diverse forms of representation and practice associated with it, conceptualize and practice a more just world broadly, while avoiding utopian determinisms and continuing to remain critical and multiple?

For more information about this series or for submission of manuscripts, please contact:
Gaile S. Cannella
gaile.cannella@gmail.com

To order other books in this series, please contact our Customer Service Department at:
(800) 770-LANG (within the U.S.)
(212) 647-7706 (outside the U.S.)
(212) 647-7707 FAX

Or browse online by series at:
www.peterlang.com